PATHWAYS TO PLURALISM

RELIGIOUS ISSUES IN AMERICAN CULTURE

ROBERT A. SPIVEY

EDWIN S. GAUSTAD

RODNEY F. ALLEN

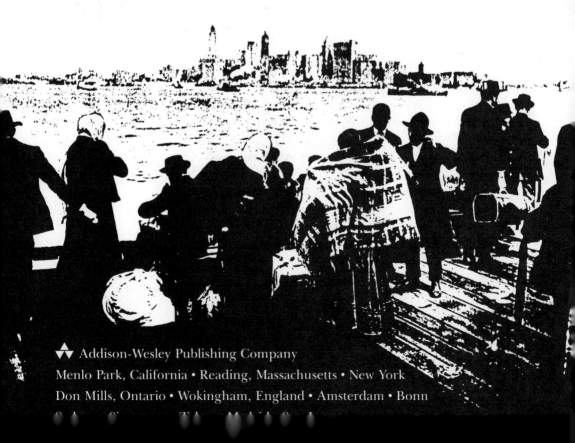

▲ Addison-Wesley Publishing Company

Menlo Park, California • Reading, Massachusetts • New York

Don Mills, Ontario • Wokingham, England • Amsterdam • Bonn

Acknowledgements:

Photographs and Illustrations:

i Library of Congress; 3 Library of Congress; 9 City of Bristol Museum and Art Gallery; 13 Courtesy of Randolph-Macon Woman's College; 14 Courtesy of the Pennsylvania Academy of the Fine Arts; 23 Virginia Gaustad; 33 Library of Congress; 36 Baptist Joint Committee; 47 Linoleum blockprint by R.O. Hodgell; 51 Keystone-Mast Collection, UC Riverside; 56 Keystone-Mast Collection, UC Riverside; 61 Library of Congress; 63 Library of Congress; 75 Library of Congress (Gordon Parks photograph); 83 A. Phillip Randolph Institute; 84 Keystone-Mast Collection, UC Riverside; 85 Religious News Service; 87 AP/Wide World; 93 Library of Congress; 95 Religious News Service; 98 Library of Congress; 103 Consulate General of Israel in New York; 109 Religious News Service; 113 National Council of Churches; 120 Keystone-Mast Collection, UC Riverside; 127 Keystone-Mast Collection, UC Riverside; 131 Religious News Service; 143 Library of Congress; 145 National Archives; 152 Keystone-Mast Collection, UC Riverside; 154 MESSENGER photo by Nguyen Van Gia; 159 Peggy Gaustad; 163 Religious News Service; 165 Pan American Union; 169 Library of Congress; 179 Keystone-Mast Collection, UC Riverside; 181 Keystone-Mast Collection, UC Riverside; 183 Religious News Service; 187 Zen Center of Los Angeles; 188 Everett C. Johnson/Folio Inc.

Maps:

19 Reprinted with permission of Charles Scribner's Sons, an imprint of Macmillan Publishing Company, from ATLAS OF AMERICAN HISTORY, edited by James Truslow Adams and R. V. Coleman. Copyright 1943, copyright renewed 1977; 52, 53, 54, 55, 57, 58, 141 From Edwin S. Gaustad, HISTORICAL ATLAS OF RELIGION IN AMERICA (New York: Harper & Row, 1962). Reprinted with permission of Harper & Row, Publishers, Inc.; 66 ATLAS OF THE HISTORICAL GEOGRAPHY OF THE UNITED STATES, by Charles O. Paullin, Carnegie Institution of Washington, D.C. and American Geographical Society of New York, 1932.

Book design and cover design by Mark O'Connor.

This book is published by the Addison-Wesley INNOVATIVE DIVISION.

ISBN 0-201-22177-2

ABCDEFGHIJKL-ML-89432109

ABOUT THE AUTHORS

ROBERT A. SPIVEY, Professor of Religion and Chancellor at Randolph-Macon Woman's College, is a graduate of Duke University, Union Theological Seminary (NY), and Yale University (1962). A former Executive Director of the American Academy of Religion, his publications include *Anatomy of the New Testament* with D. Moody Smith (Macmillan, 1982, 3rd edition) and religion materials for elementary and secondary school students.

EDWIN S. GAUSTAD, Professor of History at the University of California, Riverside, defines the religious history of America as his principal area of research. With degrees from Baylor University and Brown (Ph.D., 1951), he has written six books and edited several others. His most recent work is *Faith of Our Fathers: Religion and the New Nation* (Harper & Row, 1987).

RODNEY F. ALLEN, Professor of Social Studies Education at Florida State University, Tallahassee, is particularly interested in curriculum development with emphasis on ethics and value analysis. With degrees from the University of Delaware and Carnegie-Mellon University, he has the distinction of many successful years of teaching at both the high school and college levels. Active in the National Council for the Social Studies, he is also the recipient of awards from the Asia Society and the Fulbright-Hayes Program. His publications include *Inquiry in the Social Studies* (National Council for the Social Studies, 1968), with P.H. Lyon and J.V. Fleckenstein; *Violence and Riots in Urban America* (Wadsworth, 1969), with C.H. Adair; and *A Guide to the Bible Reader* (Bruce, 1970), with R.A. Spivey.

NOTE: An earlier version of this book was produced with support from the Danforth Foundation, St. Louis, Missouri. The authors wish to acknowledge the generous support of the Danforth Foundation and its president, Gene L. Schwilck. We also wish to acknowledge the work of Lawrence R. Hepburn, who assisted in the preparation of the Teacher's Guide that accompanied the earlier publication.

Contents

Preface to Students   *ix*

-------- STUDY 1 --------

Why Go to the New World?   *1*

INTRODUCTION   *2*

SIR HUMPHREY GILBERT

*"A Discourse on How Her Majesty
May Annoy the King of Spain"*   *4*

THE REVEREND
RICHARD HAKLUYT THE YOUNGER

"A Discourse on Western Planting"   *7*

-------- STUDY 2 --------

Conformity or Diversity?   *11*

INTRODUCTION   *12*

WILLIAM PENN

*"The Great Case
of Liberty of Conscience"*   *14*

THOMAS BARTON

*"A Letter to the Society
for the Propagation of the Gospel"*   *17*

STUDY 3

The American Revolution:
A Religious War? *21*

INTRODUCTION *22*

THOMAS BRADBURY CHANDLER
"An Appeal to the Public" *24*

WILLIAM LIVINGSTON
"A Letter to the Bishop of Landaff" *26*

STUDY 4

Subsidy or Separation? *29*

INTRODUCTION *30*

FOUNDING FATHERS DISAGREE
ON SUBSIDY FOR RELIGION *31*

TAX EXEMPTIONS FOR CHURCHES *36*

THE CHURCHES SPEAK:
FOUR POINTS OF VIEW *38*

A SUMMARY OF ARGUMENTS *44*

THE SUPREME COURT SPEAKS *46*

THE CASE OF MIDDLETOWN *48*

STUDY 5

The Churches
on the American Frontier *49*

INTRODUCTION *50*

THE CHURCHES AND THE FRONTIER *50*

RELIGIOUS INFLUENCES
ON THE FRONTIER *60*

COLLEGES AND UNIVERSITIES
ON THE FRONTIER *65*

TOWN MEETING ON THE FRONTIER *67*

STUDY 6
Black Americans and the Churches *69*

INTRODUCTION *70*

THE CHURCH AS REFUGE AND HOPE *74*

THE CHURCH DIVIDED AND REPROACHED *76*

CHRISTIANITY ABANDONED
AND CHRISTIANITY CHALLENGED *82*

STUDY 7
Religion: Personal and Social *89*

INTRODUCTION *90*

PERSONAL RELIGION *90*

HASIDISM: RELIGION — PERSONAL AND SOCIAL *102*

SOCIAL RELIGION *104*

ORGANIZED RELIGION AND AMERICAN SOCIETY *111*

MIDDLETOWN: A CASE FOR PANEL DISCUSSION *114*

STUDY 8
Ways of Understanding: Science and Religion *117*

APPROACHES TO NATURE *118*

SCIENCE AND RELIGION AT WAR *119*

CHRISTIANS DISAGREE ON DARWIN *120*

DARWIN, THE COURTS, AND THE SCHOOLS *123*

THE BIBLE AND EVOLUTION *126*

CREATIONISM AND THE CLASSROOM *129*

STUDY 9
_____

Conscience or Constitution? *133*

A MATTER OF CONSCIENCE *134*

THE MORMONS AND POLYGAMY *138*

JEHOVAH'S WITNESSES AND SALUTING THE FLAG *142*

RELIGIOUS OBJECTIONS TO WAR *151*

STUDY 10
_____

America: Protestant or Pluralist? *153*

INTRODUCTION *154*

PROTESTANT NATIVISM
AND ROMAN CATHOLIC RESPONSE *155*

ROMAN CATHOLICISM
AND ITS AMERICAN VARIETIES *162*

JEWS IN AMERICA *165*

EASTERN ORTHODOXY IN AMERICA *177*

THE ORIENT IN AMERICA *185*

PATTERNS OF PLURALISM *187*

PROBLEMS OF PLURALISM *188*

Index *195*

Preface to Students

Learning about Religion

In this book of ten studies you will learn about the place of religion in American culture. Because religion has greatly influenced the course of American history and because it continues to have an impact on American life, an examination of its role is a necessary part of social studies. In order to understand the society in which you live, you need to know something of the development of the religious ideas, practices, and institutions found in America today. It is as important to study these kinds of materials as it is to study political, military, social, and economic issues.

Social studies, indeed all formal education, is intended to help you make meaning of reality and to make judgments on issues that matter. Certainly, religion is part of reality in America and is involved in much of American history. The ten studies in this book present issues, bits of reality concerning religion and society, for which you will be asked to build explanations through personal and class inquiry. Schools in a pluralistic, democratic society can ask no less of students if their education is to be vital and complete.

Sources of Information

Each study utilizes primary sources that treat a significant religious dimension of American history. These source readings—the heart of each study—can be read at home or in class, as your teacher prefers. A set of guiding questions is provided for each reading. These questions are *not* for homework or for tests. They are designed to help you focus your reading on the major points and identify the central considerations in each reading. Each guiding question, when coupled with class discussions, will help you attain intellectual skills essential for handling historical and contemporary issues. As you learn about a particular religious issue, you are expected to draw your own conclusions on the basis of the information provided. Your teacher will evaluate your work not on the basis of the position you take, but on the basis of your thoughtful reading and careful method used in reaching that position.

Class Discussion

In preparing for class discussion you should use the guiding questions to focus your reading. Read for the main points and clusters of facts that an author presents. Take notes. If the meaning of a word is not clear, use the dictionary. Note phrases and points that are not clear so that you can raise questions in class. Even if you have your own study style, you might find the following approach helpful: 1) skim the entire reading with the guiding questions in mind; 2) read the entire article carefully, taking notes related to the guiding questions; and 3) plan some time to reflect upon the significance of the reading within the context of the study unit. In each study, you and your classmates will explore many sides of an issue. In this way, you can learn more about the problem than you would by merely answering a set of multiple-choice or essay questions. Open discussion is an essential element to understanding. It is important, therefore, to complete each reading before the class discussion begins, so that you are prepared to participate.

1

Why Go
to the
New World?

INTRODUCTION

SIR HUMPHREY GILBERT

*"A Discourse on How Her Majesty
May Annoy the King of Spain"*

THE REVEREND
RICHARD HAKLUYT
THE YOUNGER

*"A Discourse
on Western Planting"*

Introduction

Many times you have probably asked someone, "What are you doing that for?" He or she may have been doing any number of things, from studying to pacing the floor to helping with housework to teasing a friend. In each case you observed a person's actions and were interested in finding the reasons for such behavior. In some cases you were given an explanation by the individual. Sometimes, however, the answer may have been, "Oh, just because I want to," or "I don't know." And sometimes the person may have given you a false reason, not knowing or wishing to tell the truth.

Some teen-agers, for example, get summer jobs. Why? "For money, of course," you may reply. But then some of you may have friends who work even though their parents give them plenty of allowance. These teen-agers don't need to work for spending money, nor do they need to contribute to the family income. Why, then, do they work? Equally important, why do their parents often require them to seek part-time or summer jobs?

Teen-agers do other things that may lead you to ask, "Why are you doing that?" You may ask why a friend attends a summer camp and participates in athletic or club activities; why certain people are invited to a party; why your friend chooses to read certain books found on an English book-report list. In all of these cases, you want to know what *motivates* your friend to act the way he or she does.

Often it takes quite a bit of inquiring to find the reasons behind people's actions. To introduce you to the problem of determining motivation, your teacher will divide the class into groups. Each group will offer a list of possible motives for

1. Getting a summer or part-time job
2. Inviting certain people to a party
3. Reading a particular book from an English-class list

As each group presents to the class its list of possible motives, certain questions should be asked:

1. What information do you have to suggest that a particular motive lies behind the actions of your friend?
2. How might you find out what the real motive is?
3. Would it be possible for a teen-ager to get a summer job for one reason while his parents encouraged him to do so for quite a different reason?
4. Do you think most people act because of a single motive or because of a number of motives? Why?

This painting depicts the departure of the Pilgrims from Holland—first for England, then for the New World in 1620.

Historians, too, seek reasons behind human behavior. They attempt to find out why people have chosen certain courses of action. This is not an easy task, for in the past, as today, individuals often hid their motivations, and in some cases, their reasons were not completely clear to them! Thus historians must search for clues that indicate why a particular course of action was chosen. The motivation for England's entry into the New World serves as a case in point.

England Is Encouraged to Venture into the New World

In the seventeenth century, thousands of English men, women, and children left their homeland for the wild and unknown regions of America. Records of the past tell us how many people came and on what dates. We also know from which English cities they sailed and to which places in America they traveled. We know that most of them came to the New World with the special permission and encouragement of the English government. Indeed, in some cases the government even paid for people to leave their homeland.

Why did these people leave? And why was the government eager to have settlements in the New World? Sir Walter Raleigh, who was very interested in sending settlers to North America, noted that "men have traveled, as they have lived, for religion, for wealth, for knowledge, for pleasure, for power and the overthrow of rivals."

Thus, there may be many reasons for colonization. As the English wrote of the benefits to be gained from settling the New World, they had several reasons to strengthen their arguments. Often individuals' reasons were quite different from one another. Compare the following writings and note especially the motives that they reveal.

Sir Humphrey Gilbert

The first selection is from the writings of Sir Humphrey Gilbert (c. 1539–1583), the half-brother of Sir Walter Raleigh. Sir Humphrey was a daring but not particularly able seaman. After many years of effort, he finally did reach the Atlantic colonies (Newfoundland) in 1583. On his way back to England he was lost at sea. As you read what Sir Humphrey Gilbert had to say in a letter to Queen Elizabeth in 1577, keep in mind the following:

1. What is Sir Humphrey Gilbert asking permission to do? Why does he say, "I will undertake this without your Majesty's being responsible"?
2. What will be the primary gain for the English queen if Gilbert's plan is successful?
3. What arguments against his plan has Gilbert foreseen and sought to answer? Are they good answers?

A Discourse on How Her Majesty May Annoy the King of Spain[1]

The safety of nations rests chiefly in making their enemies weak and poor and themselves strong and rich. Both of these God has especially provided for your Majesty's safety if your Highness shall not pass over good opportunities for the same when they are offered. For your neighbors' misfortunes through civil wars have weakened and impoverished them both by sea and land and have strengthened your Majesty's Realm both by the one and the other—which thing is so manifest that it is vain to go about to prove the same.

[1] Adapted from D. B. Quinn, *The Voyages and Colonisation Enterprises of Sir Humphrey Gilbert* (London, 1940), Vol. I, pp. 170-75. Reprinted by permission of Cambridge University Press.

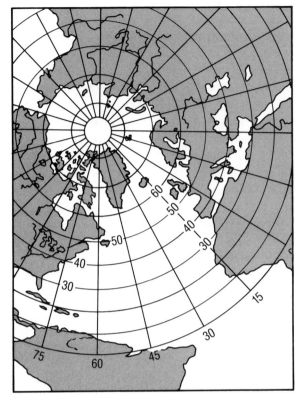

above: *Sir Humphrey Gilbert*

left: *Locate Newfoundland and England on this polar projection of the Northern Hemisphere. What parallel intersects southern England and northern Newfoundland? Why might Sir Humphrey suggest Newfoundland for his operations? Why might Denmark and Holland be good places to take captured ships?*

The way to work this feat is to set forth under a flag of discovery certain ships of war to Newfoundland. With your good license I will undertake this without your Majesty's being responsible. In the waters around Newfoundland these ships shall certainly once in the year meet all the great shipping of France, Spain, and Portugal. I would take and bring away with their freights and ladings the best of those ships and burn the worst. These captured ships I would take to Holland or Denmark or hide them as pirates for a small time upon your Majesty's coast (under the friendship of a certain vice-Admiral of this Realm[2]).

The setting forth of shipping for this service will amount to no great expense, and the return shall certainly be a great gain. For Newfoundland fish are everywhere a principal and rich merchandise that can be sold. By the gain from that, food, ammunition, and the shipping of five or six thousand soldiers can be paid for.

Some people have said, "A few shippers cannot possibly distress so many nations. Even if you take or destroy in this way all the shipping you find around Newfoundland, yet these ships belong only to the

2 Probably Sir Francis Drake.

subjects of France, Spain, and Portugal. Their own regular navy ships are not harmed thereby, so their forces will really not be diminished very much." To this argument I offer my answer.

There is no doubt that all of this can be done without danger. Although the enemies' ships may be great in number and of great burden and although they have men and munitions aboard, yet they are fishing vessels. When they come upon the coasts, they always scatter themselves into various ports. Most of the people then get into small boats for catching and drying their fish, leaving few or none aboard the ships. So there is as little doubt of easy capture and taking the ships away as there is little doubt that the power of the princely rulers will hereby decay. For the princes' own ships are very few—of small size in comparison with the others. When their subjects' ships are destroyed, it is likely that they will never be repaired. This will be true partly because of the ruin of the owners, partly through the loss of the trade that enabled them to maintain the ships. For every man who is able to build ships does not desire to use his wealth that way, so that once their shipping is spoiled, it is likely that they will never be recovered in the same number and strength. Even if they should be rebuilt, it will require a long time to season timber for that purpose, during which time we shall have good opportunity to advance our own cause. All the while these princes shall not only lose their forces, but shall also lose great revenues that by this traffic they formerly gained. As a result, they will suffer great famine for lack of the necessary victuals, etc., as they formerly enjoyed by these voyages.

Again, some have objected, saying, "Although this is a possible thing to do, it is not an allowable thing to do. It is, for one thing, against the league to which England belongs; for another, though men may not be able to see what is being done, yet unto God nothing is hidden." I answer thus.

I hold it as lawful in Christian policy to prevent a mischief in time as to revenge it too late. This is especially true seeing that God Himself is a party to the common quarrels now afoot, and the enemies' evil disposition toward your Highness and the Church is manifestly seen, although by God's merciful providence not yet thoroughly felt.

If your Majesty is willing to do all this, then I would wish your Highness to consider that delay does often times prevent the performance of good things. For the wings of men's life are plumed with the feathers of death. And so submitting myself to your Majesty's favorable judgment, I cease to trouble your Highness any further. November 6, 1577.   *Your Majesty's most faithful servant and subject,*

                                                                    H. GILBERT

The Reverend Richard Hakluyt the Younger

The second view is presented by Richard Haklyut the Younger (c. 1552–1616), who was England's most dedicated and famous advocate for the New World. In his discourses, he argued and pleaded with all who would listen, from Queen Elizabeth on down, that it was high time for England to explore and settle territory across the ocean. Richard Hakluyt was also a minister of the Church of England, and though he never personally set foot on American soil, he was named honorary minister of the first permanent English parish[3] in America at Jamestown, Virginia. As you read Richard Hakluyt's comments to the Queen in 1584, keep in mind the following:

1. What part of the New World is Hakluyt talking about? On a map, find "30 degrees in Florida northward unto 63 degrees."
2. What plan does Hakluyt have for avoiding the fate of the first Spanish missionaries in Florida? Does it make sense?
3. What is "filthy lucre and vain ostentation"? Why might Hakluyt refer to them here?
4. What chain of reasoning does Hakluyt use to support his argument that the English monarch should send preachers to the New World?

A Discourse on Western Planting[4]

The people in that part of America from 30 degrees in Florida northward unto 63 degrees (which as yet is in no Christian prince's actual possession) are idolaters, worshipping the sun, the moon, and the stars and following other forms of idolatry. It remains to be thoroughly weighed and considered by what means and by whom the most godly and Christian work of enlarging the glorious gospel[5] of Christ may be performed. By such a work, infinite multitudes of these simple people that are in error can be led into the right and perfect way of their

3 *Parish*—a geographical-ecclesiastical division within a diocese, under the supervision of a minister or priest.

4 Adapted from Charles Deane, ed., *Documentary History of the State of Maine* (Cambridge, Mass.: John Wilson & Sons, 1877), Volume II, pp. 7-12.

5 *Gospel*—literally, "good news" or "glad tidings"; the teachings of Jesus and the early apostles; any of the books (Matthew, Mark, Luke, John) detailing the life and teaching of Jesus.

salvation. The blessed Apostle Paul, the converter of the Gentiles,[6] wrote in Romans 10:

> Whosoever shall call on the name of the Lord shall be saved. But how shall they call on him in whom they have not believed? and how shall they believe in him of whom they have not heard? and how shall they hear without a preacher? and how shall they preach except they be sent?

Then it is necessary for the salvation of these poor people who have sat so long in darkness and in the shadow of death that preachers should be sent unto them. But by whom should these preachers be sent? By them no doubt who have taken upon themselves the protection and defense of the Christian faith. Now the Kings and Queens of England have the name of Defenders of the Faith. Because of this title, I think they are not only charged to maintain and favor the faith of Christ, but also to enlarge and advance it.

Now the means to send such as shall labor effectively in this business is by planting one or two colonies of our nation upon that firm land. There they may remain in safety and first learn the language of the people nearby. Little by little they can acquaint themselves with the manners of the people and so with gentleness and good judgment teach them the sweet and lively truths of the gospel. Otherwise, for preachers to come unto them rashly (without some such preparation for their safety) is nothing else but to run to their apparent and certain destruction. This is just what happened to those Spanish friars[7] who landed in Florida before any planting, without strength and company. They were miserably massacred by the savages.

Now England with her true and sincere religion proposes to plant colonies not for filthy lucre or vain ostentation, but principally for the gaining of the souls of millions of these wretched people. We would lead them from darkness to light, from falsehood to truth, from dumb idols to the living God, from the deep pit of hell to the highest heavens.

And this enterprise the princes of the religion (among whom her Majesty is principal) ought to take in hand. The Catholics convince themselves and draw others to their side, showing that they are the true Catholic church because they have been the only converters of many millions of infidels[8] to Christianity. Yes, I myself have been asked

6 *Gentile*—a non-Jew; among Mormons, a non-Mormon.

7 *Friar*—literally, "brother"; an unordained member of a Roman Catholic order such as the Franciscans or Dominicans.

8 *Infidel*—literally, "unfaithful" or "unbelieving"; generally used as a term of reproach for those not believing in a specific religion (e.g., Christianity or Islam); a pagan, a heathen.

This painting recreates the departure of John and Sebastian Cabot from Bristol, England, to the New World.

by them: how many infidels have we converted? Whereunto, although I gave the example of the ministers who were sent from Geneva into Brazil and those that went with John Ribault into Florida, as those of our nation that went with Frobisher, Sir Francis Drake, and Fenton—yet indeed I was not able to name any one infidel converted by them. But God, said I, has His time for all men; He calls some at the ninth and some at the eleventh hour. And if it pleases Him to move the heart of her Majesty to put her helping hand to this godly action, she shall find as willing subjects of all sorts as any other prince in all Christendom.[9]

Now therefore I trust the time is at hand when her Majesty's eagerness in this enterprise shall answer such objections by making possible our fruitful labor in God's harvest among the infidels. Such action will also end the many inconveniences and strife among ourselves at home in the matter of ceremonies. There are those among our clergy who by reason of idleness at home are always creating new opinions. Setting out on a voyage to lead savages to the chief principles of our

9 *Christendom*—all Christians considered as a group; also, that portion of the world or that political empire inhabited chiefly by Christians.

faith will make them less contentious and more content with the truth in religion already established by authority. So they that shall bear the name of Christian shall show themselves worthy of their vocation, so shall the mouth of the adversary be stopped, so shall contention among brethren[10] be avoided, so shall the gospel among infidels be published.

---

10 *Brethren*—though this word means simply "brothers," it is often used to refer to the members of a given religious group. There is also a Church of the Brethren, derived from a tradition of German Baptists.

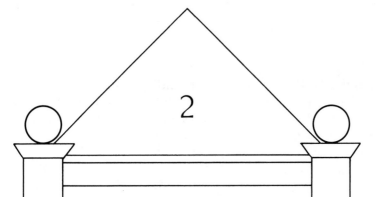

Conformity
or
Diversity?

INTRODUCTION

WILLIAM PENN
*"The Great Case
of Liberty of Conscience"*

THOMAS BARTON
*"A Letter to the Society
for the Propagation of the Gospel"*

Introduction

Initially in this study you are asked to indicate how you feel about certain issues. You do not have to sign your name and there are no right or wrong answers. Later the responses to each of the statements will be discussed.

> Read each statement carefully.
> If you *strongly agree* with it, write SA.
> If you *agree* with it, write A.
> If you are *uncertain* how you feel, write U.
> If you *disagree* with it, write D.
> If you *strongly disagree* with it, write SD.

1. Male students in high school and college should be permitted to wear moustaches and beards if they so wish.
2. In the school cafeteria, students should be prohibited from eating certain foods (such as mashed potatoes, spaghetti, and meat loaf) with their fingers.
3. The government should have the right to prohibit polygamy even if it is based on religious belief.
4. A school teacher should not be permitted to express his or her belief that Communism is desirable.
5. Uniformity in thought is necessary for a stable society.

How much should people living in a group be required to think and act just like everyone else in that group? This is the question you are asked to think about in this lesson. In the course of this study, you are encouraged to develop some thoughts of your own on the issue of *Conformity v. Diversity.*

Conformity, which may be thought of as "likeness," has been required by societies (groups) of all who become members of the group. The member is expected to think and act in a manner very similar to that which is accepted by the group as the proper or only way to think and act. Individuals who refuse to act in the proper manner are punished or driven out of the group. In small, often geographically isolated societies, maintaining conformity is not difficult. As a result, harmony and stability are noted in these societies.

However, *conformity* by itself will not provide for the growth and progress of a society. Change for the better cannot come about unless members of the group are free to some degree. They need freedom to

One artist's representation of the New World: The Peaceable Kingdom *by Edward Hicks.*

seek different ways of meeting their needs, and they need freedom to express new ideas about the nature of things. With the introduction of *diversity,* which may be thought of as "difference," groups are able to improve upon their existence. If, however, diversity is permitted to grow unchecked, the society will disintegrate through lack of common bonds. Fear of social chaos has many times resulted in governmental enforcement of conformity.

The issue of *Conformity v. Diversity* is like a thread woven through the fabric of American history. Indeed, the very first settlers of New England were individuals who had refused to conform to certain standards of their homeland. In present-day America, where many ways of thinking and behaving exist, conflicts frequently occur among citizens who hold different views. We may observe the results of this diversity in demonstrations, marches, rallies, and confrontations between people with opposing viewpoints.

Certainly, one might observe, things would run much more smoothly if everyone believed the same things. But how is this conformity to be achieved, and at what expense? And whose ideas would be chosen as the correct or proper ones?

13

This famous painting by Benjamin West shows William Penn making a treaty with the Indians in 1701.

Examine two sides of this issue as it was seen by two men in America's past. The urgent question then was conformity versus diversity in religion. The answer to that question is revealed in the later development of American life.

William Penn

William Penn (1644–1718) was a member of the Society of Friends, who were more often called by their nickname, Quakers.[1] Before he came to America in 1681 to establish his own colony (Pennsylvania), Penn was angered and dismayed to see Quakers in England being jailed, whipped, fined, or put to death for their religious beliefs. He determined that people should be free to choose their own religion and to worship in any way they wanted. (And that's just what happened in Pennsylvania.) In 1670,

1 *Quakers*—the Society of Friends (founded by George Fox in England), especially strong in colonial America in Pennsylvania and Rhode Island.

before he came to America, William Penn wrote a book giving his ideas on religious liberty. A portion of the first chapter of that volume is here for you to read. As you read, keep in mind the following:

1. For Penn, religious liberty means not only a freedom to believe a certain way, but also a freedom to do what?
2. In a similar fashion, what does Penn mean by "persecution"?
3. According to Penn, in what ways are rulers trying to assume the powers and rights of God?

The Great Case of Liberty of Conscience[2]

First, by liberty of conscience, we mean not only a mere liberty of mind, in believing or disbelieving this or that principle or doctrine. But we also believe such liberty protects a visible way of worship, a way of worship we believe to be required of us by God. If we neglect this worship for fear or favor of mortal man, we sin and are in danger of divine wrath.

Second, by restraint or persecution, we do not only mean the strict requiring of us to believe this to be true or that to be false, and upon refusal to receive the penalties given in such cases. But by those terms we mean this much: any coercion, force or hindrance which prevents our meeting together to perform those religious exercises which are according to our faith and persuasion.

We wish to put the question in this way. Is it not true that persecution against persons exercising their liberty of conscience reduces the honor of God? Does it not also defile the Christian religion, violate the authority of Scripture, and go against the principles of common reason? Finally, does it not destroy the well-being of government itself?

Concerning the honor of God, we say that restraint and persecution for matters relating to conscience directly invade the divine right, and rob the Almighty of that which belongs to none but Himself. And this we prove by five particulars.

1. If we acknowledge that our creation comes from God only, and that no other besides Himself has endowed us with those excellent gifts of Understanding, Reason, Judgment and Faith, then certain things must be true. It must be true that any earthly authority that forces us to a faith or worship not in agreement with what God has given to us invades God's rights. For He alone has authority over conscience. As

2 Adapted from *The Select Works of William Penn* (London, 1782), Vol. III, pp. 1-13.

the Bible says, "For the inspiration of the Almighty gives understanding, and faith is the gift of God."

2. Judges and kings who persecute believe that they are infallible. Protestants have denied infallibility to all but God Himself. Perhaps our judges and kings have abandoned this Protestant position. If not, we desire to know when and where they were granted the divine gift of being infallible. We also wish to know whether restraint and persecution were ever thought by God to be the fruits of His Spirit. Even that, however, is not enough. Unless *we* are convinced that these authorities are infallible (it is not enough if *they* believe it), we cannot look upon it as anything more than an anti-protestant way of believing.

3. To restrain and to persecute makes man a king over conscience. And God has reserved this to himself against all the rulers on earth. If men shall be subject to their fellow creatures regarding their bodies and souls, it follows that the ruler—Caesar—has all of God's share and his own, too! If Caesar is lord of both body and soul, then both are Caesar's and not God's.

4. Restraint and persecution defeat God's work of grace and the invisible operation of His eternal Spirit. Only His Spirit and grace can bring about faith, and only these are to be obeyed in religion and worship. Persecution makes men conform only because of outward force and bodily punishments. A faith enforced this way is subject to as many revolutions as the powers that enact it.

5. Finally, persons who persecute assume the judgment that is God's alone. Whoever holds men accountable in matters of faith, worship and conscience takes all power of judgment unto himself. But it is equally true that God shall judge all by Jesus Christ. Therefore, no man is so accountable to his fellow creatures as to be restrained or persecuted for any matter of conscience whatever.

So in this and other ways, men are accustomed to invade the divine right. At best they are misguided when they imagine that "they do God good service." Where they cannot give faith, they will use force. Yet God will not give His Honor to another. God alone grants to men the gifts of understanding and faith, and without these it is impossible to please Him.

Thomas Barton

Thomas Barton (c. 1730–1780) was a missionary from the Church of England[3] to America. He spent most of his time in William Penn's colony, where religious freedom prevailed. Barton had never before known any place where such a variety of religions existed. The variety not only existed but even seemed to be encouraged! Penn had died (1718) long before Barton arrived in Pennsylvania (1751). It is clear, however, that the views outlined in "The Great Case of Liberty of Conscience" were still being followed in the "Quaker colony." What Barton thought of all this can be found in letters that he sent back to his native England in 1762. He is addressing the head of his missionary organization, the Society for the Propagation of the Gospel in Foreign Parts. As you read, keep in mind the following:

1. What does Barton indicate has been the result of religious diversity? What assumptions does he make? What evidence does he use to support his judgment?
2. What specifically does Barton suggest the government do to bring some Pennsylvanians into the church?
3. What kind of a citizen does Barton think is best?
4. What kind of an observer do you consider Barton to be—a disinterested historian, an interested participant, or a biased or neutral reporter?

A Letter to the Society for the Propagation of the Gospel[4]

LANCASTER, PENNSYLVANIA
November 8, 1762

Reverend Sir:

. . . This mission takes in the whole of Lancaster County (80 miles in length and 26 in breadth), part of Chester County and part of Berks. So the circumference of my mission alone is 200 miles. The County of Lancaster contains upwards of 40,000 souls. Of this number not more

---

3 *Church of England*—the official and established Church in England, also known as the Anglican Church. In America, after the Revolution, the Church of England became the Protestant Epsicopal Church in the U.S.A., now simply the Episcopal Church.

4 Adapted from W.S. Perry, *Historical Collections Relating to the American Colonial Church* (Hartford, 1871), Volume II, pp. 366-368.

than 500 can be reckoned as belonging to the Church of England. The rest are German Lutherans, Calvinists, Mennonites, Moravians, New Born, Dunkers, Presbyterians, Seceders, New Lights, Convenanters, Mountain Men, Brownists, Independents, Papists, Quakers, Jews and so forth! Amid such a swarm of sects,[5] all indulged and favored by the government, it is no wonder that the National Church should be borne down. At the last election for the county to choose assemblymen, sheriff, coroner, commissioners, assessors and the like, 5000 citizens voted and yet not a single member of the Church was elected into any of these offices.

Notwithstanding these and like discouragements, I have the satisfaction to assure the Society that my people have continued to give proofs of that submission and obedience to civil authority which it is the glory of the Church of England to instill. While faction and party strife have been tearing the province to pieces, members of the Church of England behaved themselves as became peaceable and dutiful subjects, never meddling in the least.

The Germans in general are well inclined to the Church of England and might easily be brought over to it. A law obliging them to give their children an English education would soon have this effect. Such a law could not be regarded as an abridgement of their liberty since they are British subjects.

The Presbyterians are in much disrepute with all other sects and seem to be at a standstill. They gain no members except by importing from their own society in Northern Ireland. They are a people who are unsteady and much given to change, fond of novelty, and easily led away by every kind of doctrine. This disposition will ever be a bar to their increase.

The Church of England then must certainly prevail at last. She has hitherto stood her ground amid all the rage and wildness of fanaticism. While Methodists and New Lights have roamed over the country, leading captive silly women and drawing in thousands to adopt their strange and novel doctrines, the members of this Church have held fast the profession of their faith without wavering. If deprived, as the Church is, of any legal establishment[6] in her favor and remote from the immediate influence and direction of her lawful governors the

5 *Sect*—where there is an Established Church, the term *sect* designates all other religious groups. In America where there is no Established Church, *sect* has no precise meaning. It tends to be applied to smaller or younger Christian groups, while *cult* tends to be used for smaller or younger groups outside the Christian tradition.

6 *Establishment*—the formal, official, legal recognition of a specific church by the state; normally includes taxation of all citizens for the support of the Established Church.

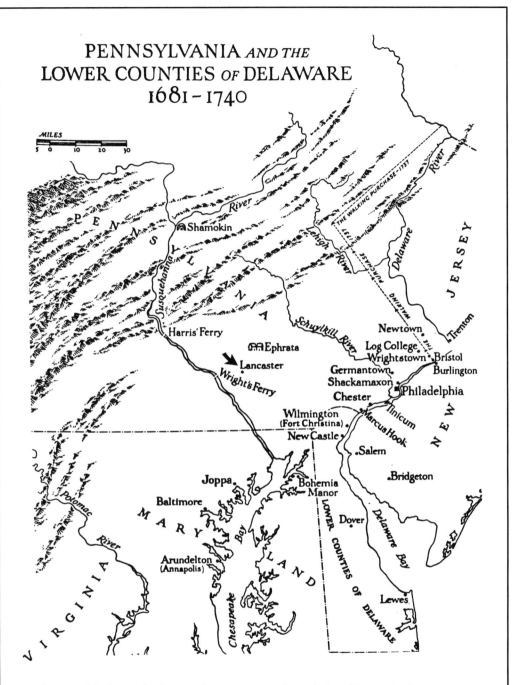

PENNSYLVANIA *AND THE*
LOWER COUNTIES *OF* DELAWARE
1681 – 1740

MILES

5 0   10   20   30

PENNSYLVANIA

Shamokin

Susquehanna River

Lehigh River

Delaware River

THE WALKING PURCHASE—1737

WALKING PURCHASE

JERSEY

Harris' Ferry

Ephrata

Lancaster

Wright's Ferry

Schuylkill River

Newtown

Log College
Wrightstown • Bristol

Germantown•   Burlington

Shackamaxon•

Chester   •Philadelphia

Tinicum

Wilmington
(Fort Christina)•

NewCastle•

Marcus Hook

•Salem

NEW

Joppa•

Bohemia
Manor

•Bridgeton

Baltimore•

MARYLAND

Potomac River

Dover•

Delaware Bay

LOWER COUNTIES OF DELAWARE

Arundelton
(Annapolis)•

Chesapeake Bay

Lewes•

VIRGINIA

At the time of the first Federal Census in 1790, the total population of Lancaster County was
36,000. This may be compared with the population of America's three largest cities at that time:
New York, 33,000; Philadelphia, 28,000; and Boston, 18,000.

bishops, she has stood unmoved and gained a respectable footing.

The establishment of bishops in America has long been talked of and long expected. This could never in any former time be introduced with more success than at present. Many of the principal Quakers wish for it in hopes it might check the growth of Presbyterianism which they dread. The Presbyterians, on the other hand, would not choose to murmur at a time when they want the assistance of the Church against the combinations of the Quakers who would willingly crush them. These things have perhaps been already mentioned to and considered by the Society. But the affection which I bear the Church of England would not permit me to omit any hint that I thought might be in advantage to her.

I am, Reverend Sir
THOMAS BARTON

3

The American Revolution: A Religious War?

INTRODUCTION

THOMAS BRADBURY
CHANDLER
"An Appeal to the Public"

WILLIAM LIVINGSTON
"A Letter to the Bishop of Landaff"

Introduction

Let all mankind know that we came into this wilderness because we would worship God without that Episcopacy,[1] that common prayer, and those unwarranted ceremonies with which the land of our forefathers had been defiled.   —COTTON MATHER, 1702

People have no security against being unmercifully priest-ridden but by keeping all imperious [domineering] bishops[2] from getting their feet into the stirrup at all.   —JONATHAN MAYHEW, 1750

Considering the encroachments that have lately been made on our civil liberties . . . is this a time to think of episcopal palaces, of pontifical revenues, of spiritual courts? . . . A Bishop would be one of the worst commodities that can possibly be imported into a new country, and must inevitably result in absolute desolation and ruin.

—An "American Whig" in a letter to the
New York Gazette, March 14, 1768

The prejudices and objections of most of our colonies are too deeply rooted and too well founded for them ever to submit quietly to an American Episcopate[3] established over them by Parliament. This would be to destroy their charters, laws, and their very constitutions.

—The "Centinel" in a letter to the
Pennsylvania Journal, March 24, 1768

A bishop and his officers, independent of the people! I tremble at the thought of such a powerful spy in a country just forming. Rouse then, Americans! You have as much to fear from a minister of the Church as you have from a minister of State.

—An "American Whig" in a letter to the
New York Gazette, April 11, 1768

What seems to be the trouble here? Are these speakers afraid of something or somebody? What? Who? Why? What are they speaking out against? Why did the letter writers want to hide their identities?

1 *Episcopacy*—refers to the group of ruling bishops and their jurisdictions.

2 *Bishop*—literally an "overseer," the bishop holds the highest of the church offices in the three ancient Christian orders: deacon, priest (or presbyter), bishop. The precise duties of the bishop vary from denomination to denomination and—to some extent—from country to country.

3 *American Episcopate*—one or more Church of England bishops residing or ruling in the American colonies.

Which of the following statements best describes the writers of the five quotations:

1. They are anti-religious.
2. They fear loss of liberty.
3. They oppose bishops but for different reasons.
4. They are in disagreement with each other.

Causes of the American Revolution

St. Peter's Parish Church in New Kent County, Virginia, was built early in the eighteenth century. George and Martha Washington were married in this parish in 1759.

That the American Revolution occurred is a widely known fact. The events of that conflict have been chronicled and set down for all to see. People agree upon *where* and *when* these events took place. Far fewer agree on *why* they happened.

In studying the causes of the American Revolution, much attention has been directed toward issues raised about taxation, Parliamentary powers, and colonial ambitions. Historians examine a wide variety of written materials, searching for insights into the thinking of colonial Americans. What were the burning issues of the day? What occupied American minds?

Many years after the Revolutionary War, the second President of the United States looked back and commented that the plan to send bishops to American in the 1760s spread a universal alarm against the authority of Parliament. It excited a general and just apprehension that bishops and dioceses and churches and priests and tithes[4] were to be imposed by Parliament . . . if Parliament could tax us, they could establish the Church of England with all its creeds, articles, tests, ceremonies and tithes.

—JOHN ADAMS, 1818, commenting on the causes of the American Revolution

4 *Tithe*—a tenth of one's income or harvest, given to support church or synagogue and its clergy.

23

If a plan so controversial was seriously considered, strong arguments favoring the plan and impassioned ones rejecting it had to exist. Two such arguments are presented below.

Thomas Bradbury Chandler

Thomas Bradbury Chandler (1726–1790) was an Anglican (Church of England) minister in Elizabethtown, New Jersey. In 1767, nine years before the American Revolution, he wrote the following *Appeal to the Public*. His aim was to persuade Americans that it was safe and fair to allow Anglican bishops to come to America. In fact, he said it was unjust and cruel to exclude them. As you read this selection, keep in mind the following:

1. What objections did Americans raise to having Anglican bishops in "this country"? How did Chandler react to these objections?
2. What is Chandler's political argument for importing bishops? Would any Americans be impressed by this position? Why? Why not?

An Appeal to the Public[5]

The arguments for sending Bishops of the Church of England to America are so strong and convincing that an Appeal may be made for the reasonableness of sending them. Nothing more than a proper explanation is necessary to recommend the sending of Bishops to the approval of every honest and unprejudiced person. Without such an explanation, many are still opposed to an American Episcopate. Some are busy misrepresenting the matter and spread their prejudices and objections against it.

That the Clergy of several of the Colonies have requested one or more Bishops to be sent to America is a matter now generally known. It was never intended to be kept as a secret. As there is great reason to hope that this request in due time will be granted, it is proper to inform all concerned why an American Episcopate is so earnestly desired by the Clergy—and by other friends and members of the Church.

---

5 Adapted from Thomas Bradbury Chandler, *An Appeal to the Public* . . . (New York, 1767).

When the case shall be duly explained and understood, no uneasiness will remain. No opposition can be formed against carrying out a plan that is so reasonable in itself, so necessary to the Church here, and so universally harmless to others of every denomination. As no invasion of the civil or religious privileges of any is intended, it is hoped that every objection—even every doubt or suspicion—will be entirely removed. . . .

Since ignorance is always suspicious, we may consider this question. "Shall we not be taxed in this Country for the support of Bishops if any are appointed?" I answer, "Not at all." But should a general tax be put upon the Country (even supposing we would have three Bishops which are the most that have been mentioned), yet I believe such a tax would be no more than four pennies in one hundred pounds. This would be no mighty hardship upon the Country. He that would worry so much about giving $\frac{1}{6000}$ of his income to *any* use does not deserve to be considered as a good subject or member of society.

But no such tax is intended nor, I trust, will be wanted. It has been proposed from the very beginning that the American Bishops be supported without any expense to the Country. A fund, accordingly, has been established for this particular purpose. For more than half a century, many worthy persons have contributed generously to the increase of it.

Another objection has been made by some persons. If Bishops are once settled in America (they say), there will be additions to their power just as soon as circumstances will permit it. What is easy and inoffensive in its beginning (they argue) will become burdensome and oppressive in the end. At this rate, however, there is no end to the raising of objections. For if every possible ill effect of a thing may be made an argument against it, nothing can escape. The truth is, men are not to be terrified or influenced by fear of what may be barely possible. They are to consider what is reasonable and proper in itself. They should consider what effects will probably and naturally follow.

That an American Episcopate is reasonable and proper in itself has, I trust, been sufficiently proved. There is not the slightest prospect at present that Bishops in this Country will acquire any influence or power except that which arises from general opinion of their abilities and integrity, and a conviction of their usefulness. Of this, no person need dread the consequences. Should the Government hereafter see fit to invest them with some degree of civil power worthy of their acceptance, it is inconceivable that any would thereby be injured. All that the happiness and safety of the public requires is that the legislative and executive power be placed in the hands of persons possessed of the greatest abilities, integrity and prudence. It is hoped that our Bishops will always be thought to deserve this character. . . .

Nor need the author use many words to prove that considerations even of a political nature are sufficient in this matter to prevail with those unmoved by other motives. The Church of England is so happily connected and interwoven with the Civil Constitution that each mutually supports and is supported by the other. Episcopacy and Monarchy are best suited to each other. Episcopacy can never thrive in a Republican Government, nor Republican Principles in an Episcopal Church. For the same reasons, in a constitutional monarchy, no form of church government can so exactly harmonize with the State as that of a limited Episcopacy.

William Livingston

William Livingston (1723–1790) was a Presbyterian lawyer in New York. He wrote one of the letters signed "American Whig." He and Chandler had several things in common. Both graduated from Yale in the 1740s, both lived most of their lives in the Middle Colonies, both died nine years after the British surrender at Yorktown, Virginia. But on the question of Anglican bishops, they had very little in common indeed! Chandler in his *Appeal* had quoted at length from an English clergyman, the Bishop of Landaff, who was an authority—he thought—on America's religious affairs. Livingston thought otherwise and wrote an angry letter to the Bishop in 1768—eight years before the Revolution.

As you read this letter (here simplified and abridged), keep in mind the following:

1. How does Livingston view the state of religion in America compared with England?
2. What does Livingston find wrong with religion in England (the wrongs he believes Americans have left behind)?
3. What need would there be for bishops to come to America, according to Livingston?

A Letter to the Bishop of Landaff[6]

My Lord,

On reading Dr. Chandler's appeal to the public, I met with a long quotation in favor of an American episcopate from a sermon preached by you. This raised my curiosity to obtain the sermon itself. And then the reading of it—your lordship will pardon me for saying—aroused at once my indignation and my sorrow. For indeed, my lord, I question whether there be a pamphlet in the nation that contains so great a number of departures from the truth as this sermon.

The passages in your sermon, my lord, which I particularly have in mind are those that relate to the American colonies. You say, "Since the discovery of the new world, the same provision has not been made of ministers necessary to the support of Christianity among those who have gone there, especially in the British colonies." This, my lord, is so contrary to the truth that the colonies do in many cases make more provision for a ministry than does any other part of the Christian world. In the New England colonies, particularly, they have from their earliest settlement been peculiarly attentive to the most ample provision for a gospel ministry. Their legislative acts abundantly show this attention. I will venture to affirm that there is not a more virtuous, not a more religious people upon the face of the earth.

Indeed, my lord, from the most authentic accounts of the state of religion in England, I have reason to think the Colonies surpass both in the theory and practice of Christianity. They surpass those enjoying the supports of a legal establishment, those who are always basking in the full sunshine of episcopal preëminence. Your lordship will readily admit that, despite all the millions spent in maintaining the Church of England, the people of England do not outshine in purity of morals persons in the protestant parts of Switzerland, in the republic of Holland, or in the church of Scotland. None of these people know anything about episcopacy, except as we do in the colonies—at a convenient and comfortable distance.

Second, my lord, in what sense can you say that the colonists have abandoned their native religion? Your lordships's charge is certainly groundless. There never was a people in the world who have been more earnest in preserving their native religion and in transmitting it, pure and uncorrupt, to their posterity. But if your lordship means by "their native religion" (1) an implicit submission to ecclesiastical-political power arbitrarily assumed and tyrannically exercised; or (2) a recognition

6 Adapted from William Livingston, *A Letter to the Right Reverend Father in God, John, Lord Bishop of Landaff*... (Boston, 1768).

of any man on earth as supreme head of the church; or (3) a superstitious attachment to rites and ceremonies of human invention to the neglect of vital piety and purity of heart, then yes, my lord. It is agreed that in this sense they did indeed abandon "their native religion." And 'tis devoutedly to be wished that their posterity may never be so infatuated as to resume it.

With this, my lord, I shall humbly take my leave. I also heartily wish that your lordship may be so thoroughly satisfied in the discharge of your episcopal function within the limits of your present diocese as never to think it your duty to exchange the See[7] of Landaff for a diocese in America!

I am, my Lord,
Your Lordship's most obedient humble servant,
WM. LIVINGSTON

---

7 *See*—a cathedral town; the charge or territory of a bishop.

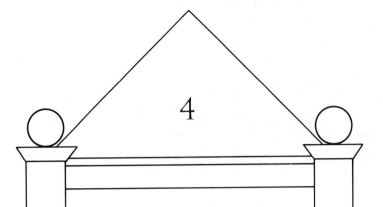

Subsidy
or
Separation?

INTRODUCTION

FOUNDING FATHERS
DISAGREE ON
SUBSIDY FOR RELIGION

TAX EXEMPTIONS
FOR CHURCHES

THE CHURCHES SPEAK:
FOUR POINTS OF VIEW

A SUMMARY
OF ARGUMENTS

THE SUPREME COURT
SPEAKS

THE CASE OF
MIDDLETOWN

Introduction

"Let's get this issue settled—now, once and for all!"

How many times have we heard that strong sentiment expressed? Perhaps, on occasion, we have even found ourselves tempted to cry out in this way. And, fortunately, such impatience often encourages an honest facing of the issue so that it does, in fact, get settled.

On the other hand, history is crammed with issues that simply refuse to stay settled. Put down in one form, they arise in another. Resolved in one generation, they reappear in the next. These are the sorts of issues that we need to know as much about as possible. Not that we are likely to settle them either, but we are likely to have to face them in some form and make some decision regarding them.

Why won't issues of this type lie down quietly or, better yet, just go away? One might suppose that it is because we all become so irrational or so emotionally involved in the issue that we cannot discuss it with any intelligence at all. Or one might suppose that the issue is really just a semantic one, merely a debate about the meaning of words. But the hard fact is that some issues persist generation after generation because the human interests they speak to are so deep, the divisions over principle or priority so sharp, that they must be dealt with over and over and over again.

Such is the issue of the proper sphere or limits of religion and of politics, or of what is often called the separation of church and state. It is an issue in twentieth-century America, but it has been an issue from the very beginning of American history. It was an issue among the Puritans in New England, among the Jews in the colony of New York, among the Catholics in Maryland, and among the Anglicans in Virginia. And it was an issue that, try though each of these groups did, was never settled.

When the thirteen colonies became a nation, they faced the hard decision of what relationship to create or allow between the new nation and the many, many churches. Should the state be an ally of the church, an enemy of the church, or entirely neutral toward the church? Should the church cooperate with the government, undermine the government, or ignore the government? These were not simple, easy-to-answer questions. And just how the issue should be settled was a complex, difficult matter. One proof of that difficulty is that even two hundred years ago, patriots of good will could not agree.

Founding Fathers Disagree on Subsidy for Religion

Patrick Henry

Patrick Henry (1736–1799) is best remembered for his stirring call to fellow Virginians—"Give me liberty or give me death!"—urging them to throw off British tyranny. Once that tyranny was thrown off in the American Revolution, many hard questions remained for the new nation to settle. What, for example, should be done about the Church of England in Virginia? It had been the official, favored church. But if you have just fought a war against England, are you likely to protect and favor the Church of England? Well, then, do you create a Church of America that will be favored above all others? Do you refuse to give special favor to any particular church? (No nation had done such a thing as that.) Or, do you support many churches equally? Here in a bill presented to the General Assembly of Virginia in 1779 we learn the position held by Patrick Henry. (Since it never passed the Assembly some of the details were left blank.) As you read, keep in mind the following:

1. How does Henry attempt to use the government to impose orthodoxy in religion?
2. How does Henry's bill tend to discourage the development of new sects or denominations?
3. What provision is made for the person not wishing to belong to a church organization?

A Bill Establishing the Christian Religion[1]

For all the encouragement of Religion and virtue, and for removing all restraints on the mind in its inquiries after truth, Be it enacted by the General Assembly, that all persons and Religions Societies who acknowledge that there is one God, and a future State of rewards and punishments, and that God ought to be publicly worshiped, shall be freely tolerated.

The Christian Religion shall in all times coming be deemed and held to be the established Religion of this Commonwealth; and all

1 Abridged from H.J. Eckenrode, *Separation of Church and State in Virginia* (Richmond, 1910), pp. 58-61.

31

Denominations of Christians demeaning themselves peaceably and faithfully, shall enjoy equal privileges, civil and Religious.

To accomplish this desirable purpose without injury to the property of those Societies of Christians already incorporated by Law for the purpose of Religious Worship, and to put it fully into the power of every other Society of Christians, either already formed or to be here-after formed to obtain the like incorporation, Be it further enacted, that the respective Societies of the Church of England already formed in this Commonwealth, shall be continued Corporate, and hold the Religious property now in their possession for ever.

Whenever (*a certain number to be fixed*) free male Persons not under twenty one Years of Age, professing the Christian Religion, shall agree to unite themselves in the Society for the purpose of Religious Worship, they shall be constituted a Church, and esteemed and regarded in Law as of the established Religion of this Commonwealth, and on their petition in Law to the General Assembly shall be entitled to be incorpo-rated and shall enjoy equal Privileges with any other Society of Chris-tians, and all that associate with them for the purpose of Religious Worship, shall be esteemed as belonging to the Society so called.

Every Society so formed shall give themselves a name or denomi-nation by which they shall be called and known in Law. And it is further enacted, that previous to the establishment and incorporation of the respective Societies of every denomination as aforesaid, and in order to entitle them thereto, each Society so petitioning shall agree to and subscribe in a Book the following five Articles, without which no agree-ment or Union of men upon pretence of Religious Worship shall entitle them to be incorporated and esteemed as a Church of the Established Religion of this Commonwealth.

First, That there is one Eternal God and a future State of Rewards and punishments.

Secondly, That God is publicly to be Worshiped.

Thirdly, That the Christian Religion is the true Religion.

Fourthly, That the Holy Scriptures of the old and new Testament are of divine inspiration, and are the only rule of Faith.

Fifthly, That it is the duty of every Man, when thereunto called by those who Govern, to bear witness to truth.

And that the People may forever enjoy the right of electing their own Teachers, Pastors, or Clergy; and at the same time that the State may have Security for the due discharge of the Pastoral office by those who shall be admitted to be Clergymen, Teachers, or Pastors, no person shall officiate as minister of any established Church who shall not have been chosen by a majority of the Society to which he shall be minister, or by the persons appointed by the said majority to choose and procure a minister for them, nor until the Minister so chosen shall have made and subscribed the following declaration, over and above the aforesaid five articles, to be made in some Court of Record in this Commonwealth, viz:

That he is determined by God's Grace out of the Holy Scriptures to instruct the people committed to his charge, and to teach nothing (as required of necessity to eternal Salvation) but that which he shall be persuaded may be concluded and proved from the Scriptures; that he will use both public and private ad-

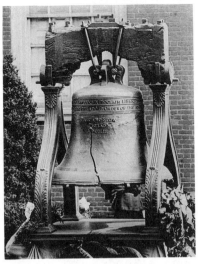

The Liberty Bell carries an inscription from the Book of Leviticus: "Proclaim liberty through all the land."

monitions with prudence and discretion, as need shall require, and occasion shall be given; that he will be diligent in prayers and in reading the Holy Scriptures, and in such studies as lead to the knowledge of the same; that he will be diligent to frame and fashion himself and his Family according to the doctrines of Christ, and to make both himself and them, as much as in him lieth, wholesome examples and patterns to the flock of Christ; and that he will maintain and set forward, as much as he can, peace and love among all people, and especially among those that are or shall be committed to his charge.

No person whatsoever shall speak anything in their Religious Assemblies disrespectfully or Seditiously of the Government of this State.

And that permanent encouragement may be given for providing a sufficient number of ministers and teachers to be procured and continued to every part of this Commonwealth.

Be it further enacted, that the sum of (*a certain amount to be fixed*) pounds of Tobacco, or such rate in Money as shall be yearly settled for each County by the Court thereof, according to the Current price, shall be paid annually for each Tithable[2] for and towards the Support of Religious Teachers and places of Worship in manner following: Within (*a certain stated number*) Months after the passing of this Act every freeholder, Housekeeper, & person possessing Tithables, shall enroll his or her name with the Clerk of the County of which he or she shall

2 *Tithable*—a person liable for the church tax.

be an Inhabitant, at the same time expressing to the Support of what Society or denomination of Christian he or she would choose to contribute; which enrollment shall be binding upon each such person, until he or she in like manner cause his or her name to be enrolled in any other Society.

James Madison

James Madison (1751–1836) disagreed very strongly and sharply with Patrick Henry. Both were patriotic Americans; both were honored Virginians. Yet they saw the question of church and state in the United States in quite different terms. Was giving state support to all Christian churches showing any favoritism? Could anyone be unhappy about receiving money from the government to advance the cause of religion? Or is the cause of religion really advanced this way? (Madison's "Memorial" was presented to the Virginia Assembly in 1785.)As you read, keep in mind the following:

1. How does Madison show his opposition to achieving religious conformity through authority? What are his reasons?
2. What is meant by taking "alarm at the first experiment on our liberties"? What is a "prudent jealousy"?
3. What, in Madison's opinion, does history teach us about "established churches" in the past? What evidence does he offer? Do you know of other historical data that would tend to support or refute his position?

A Memorial and Remonstrance[3,4]

We, the subscribers, citizens of the said Commonwealth, having taken into serious consideration, a Bill printed by order of the last Session of General Assembly, entitled "A Bill establishing ... the Christian Religion," and conceiving that the same, if finally armed with the sanctions of a law, will be a dangerous abuse of power, are bound as faithful members of a free State, to remonstrate against it, and to declare the reasons by which we are determined. We remonstrate against the said Bill,

1. Because we hold it for a "fundamental and undeniable truth," that Religion or the duty which we owe to our Creator and the manner

3 Abridged from S. K. Padover, *The Complete Madison* (New York: Harper & Row, 1953), pp. 299-306.

4 *Remonstrance*—a formal statement of complaint or protest. A memorial is a petition.

of discharging it, can be directed only by reasons and conviction, not by force or violence. The Religion then of every man must be left to the conviction and conscience of every man; and it is the right of every man to exercise it as these may dictate. This right is in its nature an unalienable right. It is unalienable; because the opinions of men, depending only on the evidence contemplated by their own minds, cannot follow the dictates of other men: It is unalienable also; because what is here a right towards men, is a duty towards the Creator.

2. Because if religion be exempt from the authority of the Society at large, still less can it be subject to that of the Legislative Body.

3. Because, it is proper to take alarm at the first experiment on our liberties. We hold this prudent jealousy to be the first duty of citizens, and one of [the] noblest characteristics of the late Revolution.

* * *

7. Because experience witnesses that ecclesiastical establishments, instead of maintaining the purity and efficacy of Religion, have had a contrary operation. During almost fifteen centuries the legal establishment of Christianity has been on trial. What have been its fruits? More or less in all places, pride and indolence in the Clergy; ignorance and servility in the laity; in both, superstition, bigotry and persecution.

* * *

11. Because, it will destroy that moderation and harmony which the forebearance of our laws to intermeddle with Religion, has produced amongst its several sects. Torrents of blood have been spilt in the old world, by vain attempts of the secular[5] arm to extinguish Religious discord, by proscribing all difference in Religious opinions. The very appearance of the Bill has transformed that "Christian forebearance, love and charity," which of late mutually prevailed, into animosities and jealousies, which may not soon be appeased. What mischiefs may not be dreaded should this enemy to the public quiet be armed with the force of a law?

After reading Madison's moving words and especially after recalling the relevant words of the First Amendment ("Congress shall make no law respecting an establishment of religion or prohibiting the free exercise thereof"), one might conclude: "Well, that issue is settled." But this conclusion would be too hasty. For if Patrick Henry lost, did James Madison completely win? Or to put the question another way: If the United States never passed "A Bill Establishing . . . the Christian Religion," did it completely renounce all financial aid to churches and synagogues? To answer

5 *Secular*—worldly or profane, as distinguished from spiritual or sacred; not religious.

Thomas Jefferson, like James Madison, argued strongly for full and complete religious liberty in Virginia and throughout America. This statue stands in his memorial in Washington, D.C.

that question with any precision or care, we must look into the whole matter of taxes. Do churches pay taxes? If so, how much and of what sort? Are taxes paid to the city or the county, to the state or to the nation? Are churches taxed on property or on income? Is a distinction made between property used for worship and property used for other purposes? Or, do churches pay no taxes? If not, why not? Is exemption granted to any institution that claims to be a church? If all churches enjoy an exemption from all taxes, then did Patrick Henry really win after all?

Clearly, this is one of those issues that will not stay settled. Does our tax policy preserve the separation of church and state? Or is tax exemption a form of subsidy? To help in the consideration of this issue, look briefly at some historical background.

Tax Exemptions for Churches

There is a fairly general agreement in the United States that the property of nonprofit educational institutions should be exempt from taxation. The same principle is applied by most Americans to churches, to church schools, and to certain other forms of church property, such as burial grounds. Such exemption from taxation is required by about one-third of our state constitutions and authorized by another third, while the remainder—mostly constitutions adopted in the early years when exemption was taken for granted—do not specifically mention the subject. These exemptions do not generally include property held for investment.

> The exemption from taxation of churches and of the land immediately about them used for church purposes is based on a European tradition going back to the fourth century, when Emperor Constantine the Great, after his conversion, gave the Church this privilege.

The grounds on which exemptions are based have been well stated in a decision of the Nebraska Supreme Court in 1890:

Exemptions are granted on the hypothesis that the association or organization is of benefit to society, that it promotes the social and moral welfare, and, to some extent, is bearing burdens that would otherwise be imposed upon the public to be met by general taxation.

The particular institution concerned in this case was the Y.M.C.A. of Omaha, but the same reasoning has often been applied in cases involving churches. . . .

The general principle of exemption of religious property from taxation is opposed by many individuals and groups on the ground that it is an indirect subsidy to religion, that even this form of aid by the State is a dangerous precedent, and that the Church would be in a stronger moral position if it gave up every form of special privilege. These opponents of exemption feel that it is inconsistent with the separation of Church and State. They acknowledge that it was justifiable in the colonies when there was an Established Church, but not today under our Federal and state constitutions. They regard it as an inheritance from colonial times without adequate present-day justification and believe that the State should be allowed to tax religious institutions if not churches themselves with a view to increasing revenue. The most important utterance by a representative public officer raising the question of possible changes in policy in this matter was by President Grant, in his seventh message to Congress. "I would suggest," he said, "the taxation of all property equally, whether church or corporation, exempting only the last resting place of the dead, and possibly, with proper restriction, church edifices." This view has a good deal of support from some secular organizations and from a few Church leaders. It has never gained large public support. . . .[6]

In the preceding historical summary you may have noted such phrases as "fairly general agreement," "most Americans," "based on a European tradition," and "opposed by many individuals and groups." These phrases, pointing to no explicit Constitutional guarantee or specific legislation, show that tax exemption for the churches is far from a clear-cut case. Historically the issue has been open to debate; currently, it is *being* debated. The several church groups themselves have been most vigorous participants in this debate, more vigorous even than the state. While the state

6 From A.P. Stokes and Leo Pfeffer, *Church and State in the United States* (New York: Harper & Row, 1964), p. 546f. Reprinted with permission of Harper & Row, Publishers, Inc.

is always in need of more revenue, the church is always in need of more souls—including its own.

The Churches Speak: Four Points of View

America

An editorial from the Roman Catholic weekly *America* reflects the views of some Catholics, though it is not an official statement of the Church. As you read the editorial, consider the following:

1. Why would the government gain no money from a tax on church income?
2. Why would a tax on church property bring little revenue?
3. Are these good arguments?

Taxing the Churches: The Law and the Facts[7]

The factual and legal sloppiness that has characterized current discussions over taxing the churches makes it necessary to recall certain truths about American law. For example, it is fatuous for anyone to assert that churches do not have to pay real estate taxes on the property they own. They do—unless they also use the property, exclusively or almost so, for religious purposes. That may be so, it will be argued, but churches do not have to pay the Federal income tax on rents they receive from property they own but lease for commercial or other nonreligious purposes.

The argument neglects to mention that, on this point, Harvard, Yale, and the Ford Foundation are in exactly the same position as the churches. Exemption of rental income is part of the general tax advantage shared by all exempt organizations. People who would take this advantage away from the churches ought to explain why they would keep it for other organizations.

The same is to be said of the proposal to tax the investment income of the churches. There might be some merit in the idea, but why

7 Reprinted with permission from *America,* June 3, 1967. All rights reserved. ©1967. America Press, Inc., 106 West 56th Street, New York, N.Y.

concentrate on the churches? The investment income of all exempt organizations is free from taxation. If we need the money badly enough to tax St. Patrick's Cathedral, Riverside Church and Temple Emmanu-El, we certainly need the money badly enough to tax labor unions, pension funds and the opulent family foundations.

The one area in which the churches have an advantage over some— but not all—exempt organizations lies in the operation of unrelated businesses. On the face of it, no exempt organization should be allowed to operate an unrelated business tax-free. Unless Congress can come up with a satisfactory reason for maintaining this peculiar exemption, the exemption ought to be phased out of our law.

Much more could be said about the realities and complexities of tax exemptions in general and of the tax status of churches in particular. Rather than get lost in technicalities, however, it will be well to turn attention to two fundamental financial questions. How much money would be realized if the income tax exemption of churches were abolished? How much money would be realized if the real estate tax exemption of churches were abolished?

Nobody knows for certain, but it is a pretty good guess that not a single penny would be realized from the abolition of the income tax exemption and that comparatively little would be realized from the abolition of the real estate exemption.

For an organization to have to pay an income tax, it must have, not an income, but a taxable income in excess of the statutory exclusions and deductions. It seems likely that the greatest part of the annual income of churches is derived from current free-will offerings. These would be excludable from taxable income of the churches because they are gifts. From their sources of income which would be classified as taxable, churches would be entitled to deduct their ordinary and necessary expenses. In view of many Supreme Court decisions in the area of Church and State, the Internal Revenue Service would have to allow churches the greatest latitude in determining what their ordinary and necessary religious expenses would be. It is wholly to be expected that every church would use up its taxable income in such expenses, with the result that churches would not have to pay any income tax at all.

So far as real estate taxation is concerned, most church property is entitled to exemption on a double ground, both as devoted to a religious undertaking and as devoted to a school, hospital, orphanage or some other charitable enterprise. It is only the houses of worship that would be substantially affected by imposition of the real estate tax. How should such property be assessed? Not on the basis of the value of neighboring commercial or industrial property, because church property cannot be used for such purposes. In all fairness, a separate basis of assessment would have to be found, one related to the economic value of the religious use of land. Since, despite the jokes, religion really isn't a profit-making affair, a fair assessment of property devoted to houses of worship probably would produce comparatively little in the way of real estate taxes.

Ultimately, the most important question is not how much money the churches have, but what they are doing with it. Part of the reason that religious organizations are given exemptions from the tax laws is that they are believed to be performing a public service. If the churches wish to keep that belief alive, they would do well to foster it not only by performing their good works in the light of day, but also by making regular, professional and informative financial reports.

General Assembly, United Presbyterian Church, U.S.A.

Unlike the *America* editorial, this Presbyterian statement is an official reaction to the tax exemption issue. As you read this statement, consider the following:

1. What does "ambiguous witness" mean?
2. What is meant by *"quid pro quo"*—especially in this context?
3. How do these two factors affect the churches' mission or work?

Relations Between Church and State

A Report to the 174th General Assembly

The United Presbyterian Church
in the United States of America, *May, 1962*[8]

I. Tax exemption for religious agencies.

The church has no theological[9] ground for laying any claim upon the state for special favors. The church must regard special status or favored position as a hindrance to the fulfilling of its mission. As a matter of contemporary fact, various levels of government give the church and many of its agencies a wide variety of tax exemptions. The church would find it difficult to obtain the abrogation of these laws

8 Excerpted from *Relations between Church and State: A Report to the 174th General Assembly* (Philadelphia, 1962), pp. 19-20.

9 *Theology*—the study of or about God; thus, the systematic presentation and interpretation of religious doctrines and speculations.

and administrative practices. In the face of this situation, two points need to be made abundantly clear by the church, the first directed to itself and its membership and the second to the state and its representatives.

First, to itself as the agent of the ministry of Jesus Christ to the world, the church should know that it renders its witness ambiguous by its continued acceptance of special privileges from the state in the form of tax exemptions. Second, the state should know that it may not expect from the church in return for favors extended of its own free will, any *quid pro quo* in the form of muting of the church's prophetic voice, nor should the state expect the church to accept the role of an uncritical instrument of support for the state's programs or of any other conscious dilution of its supreme loyalty to Jesus Christ.

In view of these considerations, the Special Committee on Church and State *recommends* that

1. The United Presbyterians study the nature of our Church's involvement in economic activity and seek ways by which it can begin the process of extricating itself from the position of being obligated, or seeming to be obligated, to the state by virtue of special tax privileges extended to it.

2. The United Presbyterian Church carefully examine its national and local related business enterprises to assure itself that under present tax laws these enterprises are not unfairly competitive with secular businesses operating in the same fields. To this end the Committee suggests that the General Assembly authorize the Stated Clerk to canvass the boards, agencies, institutions, and judicatories to determine the extent of their economic involvement subject to tax exemption and to report to the General Council of the United Presbyterian Church, which is to report to a future General Assembly.

3. The United Presbyterian Church begin efforts to obtain repeal of the section of the Internal Revenue Code that allows "churches and church organizations" exemption from the corporate income tax on profits from businesses unrelated, or only remotely related, to the purpose or activity of the church or church organizations.

4. The local churches take the initiative in making contributions to local communities, in lieu of taxes, in recognition of police, fire and other services provided by local government. This consideration commends itself especially to well-established and financially stable churches and particularly to those in communities where tax problems are developing due, in part, to the increase in exempted properties for all purposes—educational, governmental, charitable, and religious.

5. The state expect no *quid pro quo* from the church in recognition

of exemptions granted by the state; and that the church expect no *quid pro quo* from the state, as though the state owed the church some kind of special consideration in response to voluntary contributions in lieu of taxes.

Ave Maria

Published by the Congregation of the Holy Cross (Notre Dame, Indiana), *Ave Maria* presents another Roman Catholic point of view. As you read this article, consider the following:

1. Why might Congress be reluctant to condemn tax exemption for religious organizations?
2. What ethical considerations are involved in this taxation question?
3. If churches are required to pay all taxes, what might be the result?

Churches and Taxes[10]

When Congress finally gets around to serious deliberation on the tax cut, we are likely to hear some blistering speeches on the number of dollars eluding the government bite through the operation of tax-exempt foundations. (It was recently reported that the assets of these foundations last year added up to $14.5 billion.)

We shall also hear some criticism—much more cautious criticism, to be sure—about the tax dollars getting away from the government through businesses owned by religious groups. (A few months ago the *Wall Street Journal* carried a something-ought-to-be-done report on these operations. It listed church-owned holdings as diverse as hotels, supermarkets and the mortgage on Billy Sol Estes' home.)

If there should exist a Congressional district with a predominantly atheistic population, its Congressman might launch a crusade against all tax exemptions for religious organizations. But it's not likely that a majority of this Congress will push for wholesale revisions which would seriously disrupt the operations of all organized religious groups.

However, a few points should be made.

First, administrators of church property should begin to concern themselves about those holdings which are clearly tax dodges. If a business is not related to the spiritual, charitable purposes of the church; if the tax exemption amounts to an unfair competitive business advan-

10 *Ave Maria,* January 18, 1964, Notre Dame, Indiana.

tage; if the "donation" to the church isn't really a *donation* at all, but only a way in which the donor can preserve or improve his own financial situation—if these conditions are present, then the ecclesiastical administrators should be concerned about scandal and about responsibility to the nation.

Second, it should be remembered by Congressional speechmakers and by others that most of the churches, in their administration of these funds, are simply serving as agents for a very widespread membership. The taxpayers of the nation are basically the same people who are contributing to the charitable and devotional[11] works of the church. Restrictions that place harsh financial burdens on the churches are likely to curtail social services (which will fall to the responsibility of government), or they will place additional expenses on the church members. And these are the people who were supposed to benefit from tax reductions.

Finally, we accept the fact that huge networks of church-sponsored institutions resting on the shaky financial structure of tax loopholes is a situation far from desirable.

We would recommend the initiation of informal discussions between Church spokesmen and government officials to begin a gradual solution of a situation which could grow into a serious problem for all the churches.

General Convention, American Lutheran Church

This Lutheran statement constitutes another official denominational reaction. As you read these three paragraphs, consider the following:

1. How can tax policies or tax law encourage persons to give to churches and synagogues?
2. What kind of tax exemption should churches have? What kind should they not have?

Policies Respecting Taxation[12]

Tax policies should encourage personal contributions to voluntary, not-for-profit organizations of a charitable, health, educational, or religious

---

11 *Devotional*—worshipful; prayerful; having to do with acts of piety or devotion.

12 A policy statement of The American Lutheran Church included in the statement "Church-State Relations in the U.S.A." approved by the Third General Convention, October 25, 1966.

character. The community needs strong organizations of this type, alike for their positive values, to avoid total reliance upon governmental agencies, and for the mutually healthy and corrective influence between governmental and voluntary agencies. The freedom of the individual citizen to exercise his personal philanthropy and generously to support constructive voluntary enterprises of his own choice ought to be protected in the public interest.

Tax exemption of church buildings owned and used directly and solely for worship, educational, and eleemosynary[13] purposes is a sound exercise of public policy. It recognizes the contributions the church and its institutions make to community life. To levy upon churches nondiscriminatory charges for municipal services such as water, sewage, police, and fire protection we believe is an action consistent with sound public policy. We believe that the churches should be willing to accept equitable taxation of parsonages and other dwellings owned by churches, associations of churches, or religious orders in which their staff members reside.

Churches owning properties and conducting business not exclusively and solely essential to their religious, charitable, or educational ministry ought to be subject to tax laws and policies equally applicable to those governing profit-seeking individuals, partnerships, and corporations.

A Summary of Arguments

Some common arguments for and against changes in church tax exemption policies are listed below. As you examine the arguments, do the following:

1. Choose those arguments you believe to be the strongest. Be prepared to explain and defend your choices.
2. Choose those arguments you believe to be the weakest. Be prepared to explain and defend your choices.

This summary is adapted from a booklet issued by the National Conference of Christians and Jews in 1963.[14]

13 Eleemosynary—having to do with alms or almsgiving; charitable.

14 Andrew D. Tanner, *The Question of Tax Exemption for Churches*. See also Dean M. Kelley, *Why Churches Should Not Pay Taxes* (New York, 1977).

Arguments for removing or modifying tax exemption for the churches:	*Arguments against removing or modifying tax exemption for the churches:*
1 Tax exemption has no scriptural justification.	**1** The state should not tax the church because "the power to tax is the power to destroy."
2 Tax exemption is a subsidy as real as if government made a cash gift equivalent to the amount of unpaid taxes.	**2** Income from church-owned businesses is used for worthy causes, and the cost of operation of the churches is thereby reduced.
3 As the wealth of the churches grows, so hostility toward institutional religion in America will grow.	**3** Exemptions are granted to other charitable, fraternal and educational institutions; churches should not have to surrender their tax benefits while such benefits continue to be extended to others.
4 When church members lose the spirit of voluntary giving, the spiritual life of the church is weakened or it may even die.	**4** Congress has granted exemption to many organizations "in recognition of the benefit which the public derives." As long as such benefit to the public continues, churches are entitled to the same privileges as others.
5 When churches enjoy tax exemption in the operation of businesses unrelated to actual worship, then they are in unfair competition with private enterprise.	**5** Economic wealth and power is found more in tax-exempt foundations and charities than in the synagogues and churches.
6 Tax exemption for the churches is a violation of the principle of separation of church and state.	

The Supreme Court Speaks

The Constitution of the United States contains no statement whatsoever concerning tax exemption for the synagogues and churches of America. Why, then, have such exemptions been granted? The answer must be in at least three parts: 1) There is a strong tradition in Western Civilization going all the way back to the fourth century A.D. of tax exemption for religious institutions; 2) Churches, like schools, hospitals, and other non-profit institutions, are generally believed to render socially valuable functions deserving of governmental noninterference; and 3) The spirit of the Constitution if not the letter appears to support this long-standing practice.

That spirit, so far as religion is concerned, is embodied primarily in the First Amendment: "Congress shall make no law respecting the establishment of religion or prohibiting the free exercise thereof . . ." Now we often read—or even repeat—this important sentence without thinking carefully of its meaning. We may even suppose that the second clause about free exercise is merely a restatement of the first clause about establishment. But if we examine the language closely, we observe that this is not so. The clause prohibiting establishment says in effect: Congress shall not promote or sponsor religion. The clause guaranteeing free exercise of religion says in effect: Congress shall not prohibit or interfere with religion. The two clauses, thus, move in opposing directions; sometimes the ground left between them is very tiny indeed. The Constitution permits that which on the one hand will not promote religion but which on the other hand does not interfere with its free exercise. This is a tightrope, as Chief Justice Burger remarked in 1970, that the Supreme Court—and the country—must try to walk.

In May, 1970, the Supreme Court handed down its long-awaited decision in a case dealing directly with the tax exemption question. Frederick Walz, a citizen of New York City, owned a small parcel of land on Staten Island on which he paid an annual property tax of $5.24. He contended that his tax bill was higher than it would be if all the churches were required to pay property taxes, too. He was not only being penalized financially, he argued, but was also in effect helping to support or subsidize the churches and synagogues of New York City. The amount of money involved in Mr. Walz's case was, of course, quite small. But the principle involved was quite large, and this is why the Supreme Court agreed to hear the case. What did the Court say?

By a vote of seven to one, the Court upheld the long tradition of granting tax exemption to church property. The one dissenter, Justice

William Douglas, argued that tax exemption was in fact a subsidy and that while organized believers did not have to pay real estate taxes, "non-believers, whether organized or not, must pay the real estate taxes." The majority opinion of the Court, written by Chief Justice Warren Burger, contended on the other hand that removal of the tax exemption would be equivalent to requiring the churches to support the government. ". . . we have been able to chart a course that preserved the autonomy and freedom of religious bodies while avoiding any semblance of established religion. This is a 'tightrope' and one we have successfully traversed." Taxation, the Court declared, will create more involvement between church and state than does exemption.

THE
RELIGION
BU$INESS
ALFRED BALK

What symbolism do you find in this illustration?

As you read the brief excerpt from the Court's decision given below, consider the following questions:

1. Do you agree with the Court's understanding of the basic purpose of the First Amendment? Explain your answer.
2. What do you understand by the phrase "benevolent neutrality"? Does this seem reasonable to you as a path for the country to try to follow—or not?
3. Would you expect other cases involving tax money and religion to come before the Supreme Court? Why or why not?

The course of constitutional neutrality in this area cannot be an absolutely straight line; rigidity could well defeat the basic purpose of these provisions, which is to insure that no religion be sponsored or favored, none commanded, and none inhibited. The general principle deducible from the First Amendment and all that has been said by the Court is this: that we will not tolerate either governmentally established religion or governmental interference with religion. Short of those expressly proscribed governmental acts there is room for play in the joints productive of a benevolent neutrality which will permit religious exercise

to exist without sponsorship and without interference. (397 U.S. 644)
Walz v. Tax Commission of the City of New York (1970).

The Case of Middletown

The citizens of Middletown are upset about a sharp rise in their property taxes. True, the city has increased its welfare services; raised the wages of the police, fire fighters, and other city employees; and expanded the municipal utilities system, but some residents feel the tax structure is unfair.

At a meeting of the "Taxpayers' Association," the city tax assessor explains that 40 percent of the real estate within the city limits is tax exempt. These exempt properties include many nonprofit corporations and schools as well as city, state, and federal properties. Also included are churches and synagogues (some of which have large education and recreation wings), two church affiliated colleges and a seminary, a convent, two church-run hospitals, a church-owned retirement hotel, two dozen parsonages and a bishop's residence, a diocesan office building, and several parochial schools. In addition, there are church-owned parking lots, playgrounds, and cemeteries.

The assessor suggests that individual property taxes could be reduced if these exemptions were eliminated. He further states that the city has not considered doing so because the elected officials fear a strong reaction from church members. As yet, no one, he notes, has complained to the assessor's office about tax exemptions for churches.

Hearing all this, some of the citizens who also happen to be church members meet one night to discuss the question of exemptions. They are particularly concerned about the exemptions their own churches enjoy. Some favor giving up all tax exemption, but others maintain that exemptions are necessary for their churches to survive. Others argue that necessary or not, tax exemption is a desirable policy for many reasons.

Assignment: Reconstruct the meeting. What questions would be raised in the discussion? What questions might individuals have personally to resolve in choosing a position on the exemption issue? What arguments might appeal to them as citizens, as tax payers, as church members? As you prepare for the discussion, review the background article by Stokes and Pfeffer and the four church viewpoints. Look through the arguments listed by the National Conference of Christians and Jews. Then develop your own position on the issue. In between wholesale elimination or complete retention of present tax exemption practices, many intermediate positions can be defined. Also, be sure to note what other property in the city *besides* religious property is often tax-exempt.

5

The Churches
on the
American Frontier

INTRODUCTION

THE CHURCHES
AND THE FRONTIER

RELIGIOUS INFLUENCES
ON THE FRONTIER

COLLEGES AND UNIVERSITIES
ON THE FRONTIER

TOWN MEETING
ON THE FRONTIER

Introduction

Following a successful separation from England in 1783, the young new nation of United States found the doors to western expansion suddenly opened. The Allegheny Mountains that had been both a natural and a political barrier ceased to be either. As a result, settlers in their Conestoga wagons, on horseback, or on foot made their way into a beckoning West.

By the last decade of the eighteenth century, thirteen states had ratified the Constitution. A generation later, in 1821, the number of states had grown to twenty-four. In 1803, Thomas Jefferson doubled the territory of the United States with the magnificent Louisiana Purchase. Sixteen years later, in 1819, Spain sold Florida to the United States. And in 1846, a treaty between Great Britain and the United States, followed by the Mexican War, thrust American sovereignty all the way to the Pacific Ocean.

In the span of only two generations, Americans migrated from one great ocean to another. The obstacles seemed almost as large as the opportunities. Foreign powers crowded around, Indians understandably resisted, starvation and despair threatened. Even in the best of circumstances, there was much to be done: land to clear and cultivate, forts and roads to build, shops and markets to set up, schools and churches to establish. In moving out into a savage wilderness, men and women did not want to leave all civilization behind. Could people settle in the wilds without themselves becoming wild? Could morality and public order exist even on the frontier? These questions were frequently raised. Just as frequently, the churches were regarded as the key to answering these questions. How much were the churches a part of the expansion of America? How much difference—and of what sort—did their presence make?

To answer these questions, let us examine two kinds of data. First, we will look at some 1850 maps to discover which churches expanded along the frontier and where they were most numerous. Second, we will read the testimony of four men regarding the work and the promise of religion in the West.

The Churches and the Frontier

To gain information about the location and magnitude of church activity on the frontier, we can first turn to maps. (Later, information about the nature of church activity will be gained from other sources.) The maps

The religion of both Indian and Eskimo left enduring marks on the American landscape. This totem pole is located in Wrangell, Alaska.

present a county-by-county survey of the number of churches of different religious groups. Each map shows where and approximately in what numbers Baptists, Catholics, Methodists, etc., were to be found in the year 1850—a time of great expansion to the West.

These maps show the number of churches in each county by gradually darker shadings. For example, if a county on a map showing Lutheran expansion is white or blank, no churches of this faith were found in that county in 1850; if lightly shaded, a few were found; if heavily shaded, many were found. This method of giving information not only tells us where and how many churches were found, but also quickly reveals any patterns of settlement that may exist.

Though a map may tell us where, how many, and even, perhaps, in what pattern churches expanded, it does not always tell us *why* they developed where they did. One clue to this question may be provided by a topographical, or physical, map that tells us about landforms and natural conditions that can affect migration and settlement. Therefore, as you study each of the maps showing religious expansion, it would be wise to relate these patterns to the physical conditions shown on a wall map or desk atlas. Of course, there are many other reasons why churches grew as they did, and we must look to sources other than geography for this information.

As you study each map certain questions should be considered:

1. Where was this church found?
2. In what numbers was it found?
3. What patterns of growth may be seen?
4. What natural or geographical conditions may account in part for this?

Baptist Churches in 1850

1. In what parts of the country were the greatest concentrations of Baptist churches found?
2. From New York south, were the Baptists generally more prominent in coastal or interior regions? Were they more prominent in rural areas or around cities? (Check a map showing cities.)
3. By 1850 where had Baptists crossed the Mississippi River in significant numbers?
4. What might account for the heavy settlement of Baptists along the South Carolina-Georgia border?

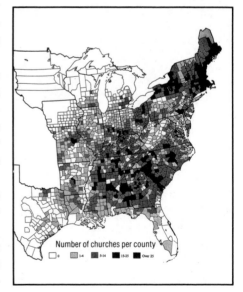

Number of churches per county

Baptist Churches: 1850

Congregational[1] Churches in 1850

1. In 1850 most Congregational Churches were found in what seven states?
2. From its New England origin, in what direction did Congregationalism expand?
3. How might the one South Carolina congregation have traveled from Massachusetts? (It did so at the end of the seventeenth century.)

Episcopal[2] Churches in 1850

1. The Episcopal Church was the official or established church of the southern colonies. By 1850 is there still evidence of their early favored position? If so, where?
2. Where were the major settlements along the Mississippi River? What cities are here?
3. Judging from this map, how successful was the Episcopal Church on the frontier?

1 Now the United Church of Christ.

2 The Episcopal Church in the colonial period was the Church of England (Anglican).

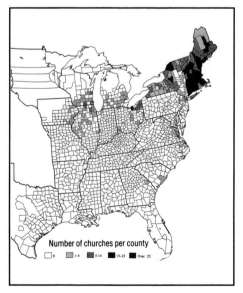

Congregational Churches: 1850   Episcopal Churches: 1850

Lutheran Churches in 1850

1. Judging from the map, at what port (the major ones were Boston, New York, Philadelphia, and Charleston) did most settlers of the great eighteenth century Lutheran migrations land?
2. From that port city, in what direction did the (German) Lutheran churches move?
3. What might account for the line of churches south from the panhandle of Maryland through Virginia?
4. Where might Lutherans coming from Europe have entered the Deep South?

Methodist Churches in 1850

1. Though Methodism arrived late in America (that is, during the Revolutionary Period itself), it was quite strong by 1850. In what states bordering the Atlantic was this true?
2. Locate the Ohio River. Could you defend the statement that "this was a highway of migration for Methodists"?
3. Compared with maps you have already seen (for example, that of Congregational churches), what does this one show you about the strength of Methodism on the frontier?

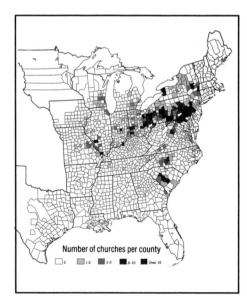

Lutheran Churches: 1850

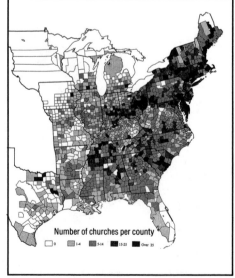

Methodist Churches: 1850

Presbyterian Churches in 1850

1. Presbyterians did not arrive in great numbers in America until the eighteenth century. From looking at this map, what evidence is there that they located on uncrowded and cheaper land farther west?
2. Using a topographical map, trace the migration from central Pennsylvania through Virginia to eastern Tennessee. What effect might topography have on settlement and thus the establishment of churches?
3. Presbyterians and Congregationalists cooperated in much of their home mission effort to win the West. Compare the 1850 maps of these two groups. Which group was more successful? What might be an explanation for this?

Quaker Churches (Friends Meetings) in 1850

1. While Quakers did not ever become a large group in America, they were a quite important group in the early history of the country. What is sometimes called the Quaker State? Why?
2. Locate Rhode Island on the map. What aspects of this colony's early history could help account for the Quaker concentration there?

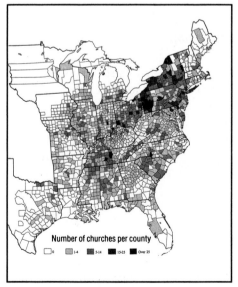
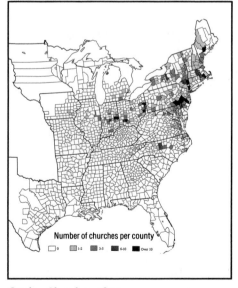

Presbyterian Churches: 1850   *Quaker Churches: 1850*

San Xavier del Bac Mission, near Tucson, Arizona, around 1900.

3. Some important Quaker colleges today are Haverford and Swarthmore (in Pennsylvania), Guilford (North Carolina), and Earlham (Indiana). From looking at this map, where in the states indicated would these schools probably be found?

Roman Catholic Churches in 1850

1. One of the thirteen colonies was founded by Roman Catholics from England. From looking at this map can you tell which colony it was?
2. The eastern half of Canada was French and Catholic. What evidence can you see of the influence of Canadian Catholicism in the United States?
3. In the eighteenth century, French Catholics were quite active in the Mississippi Valley. What signs of this can be seen?
4. Alone among America's major religious groups in 1850, the Roman Catholics had significant church strength *west* of the Mississippi River. What might account for this?

New Churches in the American West

In addition to the successes of the eastern churches moving into the West, the American frontier gave birth to new religious groups and movements.

The two most successful were the Disciples of Christ and the Mormons, officially known as the Church of Jesus Christ of Latter-day Saints.

The Disciples of Christ arose out of the doctrines and labors of such men as Barton Stone in Kentucky and Alexander Campbell of western Pennsylvania—later of West Virginia. Both men believed that denominational divisions were overemphasized. They wished to return to a simple, original Christianity of the New Testament. They wanted to be known, therefore, merely as disciples of Christ. In the mid-nineteenth century, Alexander Campbell himself described the spread of the Disciples' movement. His comments show just how western the group was, for three fourths of all members were in six states: Ohio, Indiana, Illinois, Missouri, Kentucky, and Tennessee. On the map your teacher gives you, trace a line around these six states.

1. How many are among the thirteen original colonies?
2. How many touch the Atlantic coast?
3. How many in 1850 might be regarded as frontier states?

Though the Mormon movement formally began in New York in 1830, it quickly spread toward the West. In the 1830s the group was partly in Ohio, partly in western Missouri. From 1840 to 1844, Joseph Smith watched over his followers in Illinois. The major settlement was on the

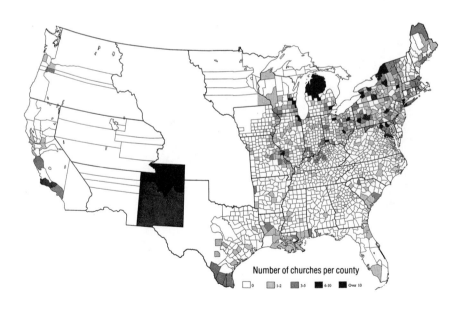

Roman Catholic Churches: 1850

Mississippi River, just across from the Iowa-Missouri line. Following the assassination of Joseph Smith in 1844, the Mormons began a long, painful journey toward the great western plains and deserts. In 1847 under the leadership of Brigham Young, they founded Salt Lake City, which was to become the great center of this now thoroughly western church. In looking at a map for 1950 (there was too much movement for one in 1850!), you can see this church as a feature primarily of the western landscape.

What enabled this church to expand so powerfully in and around Utah?

Judaism on the Frontier

In 1850, Judaism was just beginning to grow rapidly in America. Despite the modest number of Jews in America at this time, the frontier already proved attractive to some, and in Ohio particularly, Judaism and the American frontier significantly influenced each other. There, Rabbi Isaac Mayer Wise (1819–1900) labored in the 1850s and beyond, eventually founding the Hebrew Union College in Cincinnati in 1875. It has remained the major institutional center for Reform Judaism[3] in America.

3 A liberalizing movement that modified many of the ritual and legal demands of traditional Judaism. It was led largely by Jews emigrating from Germany.

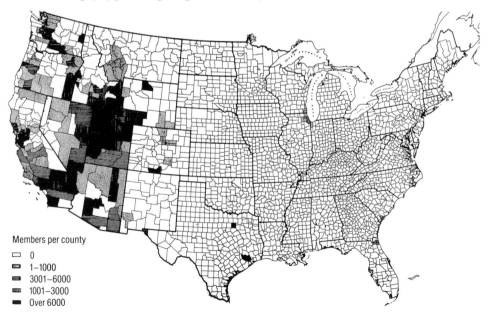

Members per county
- ☐ 0
- 1–1000
- 3001–6000
- 1001–3000
- Over 6000

Church of Jesus Christ of Latter-day Saints: 1950

The official United States census for 1850 lists only thirty synagogues in the entire country. Though recent careful research shows this number to be too low—probably it was closer to fifty—nevertheless, Judaism still represented a relatively small group in America. Most of America's synagogues were in the East, of course, particularly in such states as Pennsylvania and New York. Old colonial sites such as Newport, Rhode Island, and Charleston, South Carolina, also represented major centers of strength and continuity. In spite of its small numbers, Judaism moved out along the frontier. Synagogues were found at least in the following Western outposts: Louisville, Kentucky; New Orleans, Louisiana; St. Louis, Missouri; and Ohio, one in Cleveland and two in Cincinnati.

Immigration to America created one set of problems, and migration to a lonely western frontier could easily create another set. For a group of people long confined to European ghettos or long the victims of banishment and exile, there were still more problems. These are briefly noted in a book dealing with *American Jewry and the Civil War*.[4] The selection following is adapted from the first chapter of that book. As you read it, consider the following questions.

1. Why, even in the West, did Jews tend to prefer the city to the farm?
2. What is meant by the phrase "hemmed in by medieval restrictions"?
3. Would the American frontier be likely to have "discriminatory regulations"? Why or why not?

The urban tendency of American Jews had already become a fixed pattern by 1860. European tyrants had prohibited Jews from owning land through too many centuries for many of them to think of tilling the soil. Also, as a religio-cultural minority they were naturally inclined to dwell together in order to preserve their religious practices and worship.

The immigrants of the pre-Civil War era were faced with the necessity of adjusting themselves to a strange new civilization. Practically all of them came from lands where the life of the Jew was hemmed in by medieval restrictions. Not only were the rights of citizenship denied them, but freedom of residence, of travel, of education, of occupation, of religious expression—all of these facets of life were subject to discriminatory regulations. Jews suffered all of the disabilities of their neighbors as well as many others designed especially for them. Large numbers of those who came to America had fled from Europe not only for materialistic reasons, although they were human enough to hope for

4 By Bertram W. Korn, Copyright 1951 by The Jewish Publication Society of America. Reprinted in a paperbound edition by Atheneum Publishers, Inc., 1970.

a good livelihood, but even more because they despaired of achieving any kind of equality with their neighbors under the rotting political systems of a reactionary Europe. Practically all of the immigrant Jews came to the United States to taste the nectar of the freedom which was denied them in their native lands.

Religious Influences on the Frontier

Now that we have had an opportunity to see which churches moved with the frontier and into the West, other questions arise. What difference did the churches make? How much influence did they exercise in bringing civilization and morality to rude and rough frontier areas? How necessary were they to keep men, women, and children from falling into illiteracy and savagery?

To help answer these questions, we will look at four testimonies out of the West. They will tell us something of what the churches could do or were doing. (The language in each case is somewhat simplified.)

Lyman Beecher

The father of Harriet Beecher Stowe, Lyman Beecher (1775–1863) was a Congregationalist minister from Connecticut who decided in 1832 to move west, in this case Cincinnati, Ohio. The paragraphs following are from his book *A Plea for the West*, published in Cincinnati in 1835. As you read the selection, consider the following questions:

1. When Beecher speaks of the East aiding the West, does this give you some hint of whom he hopes this *Plea* will reach?
2. What does Beecher think will happen to the West if religion does *not* keep up with the advancing frontier?
3. What sort of aid might he seek?

All at the West is on a grand scale. Already, where churches are formed, they give more liberally than churches of the same relative condition in the East. So it is not selfishness that makes it necessary for the East temporarily to aid the West. One must consider the mighty resources of the West will be worse than useless without the influence of God and His churches.

The capacity of the West for self-destruction—without religion and moral culture—will be as terrific as her capacity for self-preservation will be glorious—*with* religion and moral culture. All of the moral energies of God's influence over men are closely associated with His ministers and His churches. The sabbath and the preaching of the gospel are Heaven's chosen instruments for bringing about a happy social state. Ignorance, vice, and superstition surround evangelical institutions, ready to rush in whenever their light and power are extinct.

John Mason Peck

A Baptist missionary to the Mississippi Valley, Peck (1789–1858) was especially interested in keeping the educational level of the frontier as high as primitive conditions would permit. In 1823 he wrote to the Massachusetts Baptist Missionary Society for help. As you read, consider the following questions:

1. What interest does this missionary have in education? Why?
2. Why did people hear preaching only once a month?

The Methodist Circuit Rider was a principal instrument for advancing evangelical religion on the American frontier.

My own experience has convinced me completely that there are important advantages which will come from the creation of Bible societies. Other societies as well could aid in the distribution of mission pamphlets, magazines and tracts. Friends in Boston could greatly help the Christian cause if they would supply me with an additional quantity of back numbers of mission magazines, missionary reports, old sermons, tracts and everything of that sort which could be distributed without charge.

These should be packed in a box marked with my name, the freight paid to New Orleans, and then directed to the charge of A. Skinner, St. Louis. I have found the most beneficial effects from distributing a few magazines or tracts after preaching. As the people in all the settlements seldom hear preaching but once a month, these silent teachers serve to keep alive impressions and feelings till the return of the preacher.

Peter Cartwright

Probably the most famous of the Methodist frontier preachers, Cartwright (1785–1872) vigorously opposed slavery, drunkenness, and gambling. With equal vigor, as this passage from his *Autobiography* (1856) shows, he supported the revivals[5] and camp meetings. As you read the passage, consider these questions:

1. What other attraction, besides religion, might bring several hundred people of the frontier together for a four or five day camp-meeting?
2. On the basis of Cartwright's testimony, how successful were revivals and camp-meetings in making new converts?

From 1801 on, a blessed revival of religion spread through almost the entire inhabited parts of the West: Kentucky, Tennessee, and the Carolinas. It spread especially through the Cumberland country, which was so called from the Cumberland River which headed in Kentucky, but in its great bend circled south through Tennessee, near Nashville. The Presbyterians and the Methodists in a great measure united in this work. They met together, prayed together, and preached together.

Our camp-meetings originated in this revival. In both these denominations[6] camp-meetings were held every year, and indeed have been ever since, more or less. Men would erect the camps with logs, and cover them with clapboards or shingles. They would also erect a shed, sufficiently large to protect five thousand people from wind and rain, and cover it with boards or shingles. They would build a large platform and benches in the shed, and here people would collect from forty or fifty miles around—sometimes farther than that. Ten, twenty, and sometimes thirty ministers of different denominations would come together and preach night and day, four or five days together. Indeed, I have known these camp-meetings to last three or four weeks, and great good has resulted from them.

I have seen more than a hundred sinners fall like dead men under one powerful sermon.[7] I have seen and heard more than five hundred

5 *Revival*—A series of preaching services, designed to win new converts and arouse old ones to new heights of devotion.

6 *Denomination*—a naming or a name; in a religious context, a specific group or body of worshippers—as the Methodist denomination.

7 *Sermon*—the religious discourse, speech, or exhortation delivered by a clergyman, usually in the context of a service of worship.

Christians all shouting aloud the high praises of God at once. And I will venture to assert that many happy thousands were awakened and converted to God at these camp-meetings. Some sinners mocked, some old dried up Christians opposed, and some of the old starched Presbyterian preachers spoke against these camp-meetings, but still the work went on. It spread in almost every direction, gathering additional force, until our country seemed all coming home to God.

Pierre Jean DeSmet, S.J.

As a missionary for the Society of Jesus, this able and earnest Catholic priest became the Indians' defender, protector, and friend. In the process, Father DeSmet (1801–1873) also became a defender and peacemaker for the white man. In the tragic tensions between advancing whites and retreating Indians, Father DeSmet was often the only man trusted by both sides. The priest agreed to help the United States Government in its peace negotiations because this duty was not "contrary to my duties as a missionary . . . as my only object is to be of use to the whites and still more to the poor Indians." How well he succeeded may be judged from a letter written by Major General David

Father Pierre Jean DeSmet, member of the Society of Jesus and able missionary to the Indians of the western plains.

S. Stanley, United States Army, to Father DeSmet's ecclesiastical[8] superior. The letter is dated July 12, 1864, and was written at Fort Sulley, Dakota Territory. As you read the letter consider the following questions:

1. On the basis of General Stanley's letter, what could you conclude about the relationship between the Indians and at least some missionaries?
2. Also judging from the letter, what larger role in American history do you see some of the frontier priests or preachers having?

8 *Ecclesiastical*—of or pertaining to a church.

Monsignor:

Herewith I send you a testimonial which the Peace Commission, lately meeting at Fort Rice,[9] has given to our well-beloved missionary, Father P.J. DeSmet.

Probably you are informed in regard to the work of this commission during the last year. In the month of May of the current year the commission succeeded in meeting at Fort Laramie, on the Platte river, a certain number of chiefs belonging to the most formidable and most warlike tribes. The Hunkpapas, however, still refused to enter into any arrangement with the whites, and it is unnecessary to say that no treaty with the Sioux was possible, if this large and hostile tribe was unwilling to concur in it. In this condition of affairs, the Reverend Father DeSmet, who has consecrated his life to the service of the true religion and of humanity, offered himself. Despite his great age, he would endeavor to penetrate to the hostile camps and to induce them to appear before the commission at Fort Rice. As the letter of the members of the commission will inform you, there is reason to believe that his mission has been wholly successful.

I could give you only an imperfect idea of the sufferings and dangers of this journey, unless you were acquainted with the great plains and the Indian character. Father DeSmet, alone of the entire white race, could penetrate to these cruel savages and return safe and sound. One of the chiefs, in speaking to him while he was in the hostile camp, told him, "if it had been any other man than you, Black-robe, this day would have been his last." . . .

The Reverend Father is known among the Indians by the name of "Black-robe" and "Big Medicine Man." When he is among them he always wears the cassock[10] and the crucifix. He is the only man for whom I have ever seen Indians show a real affection. They say, in their simple and open language, that he is the only white man who has not a forked tongue; that is, who never lies to them. The reception that they gave him in the hostile camp was enthusiastic and magnificent. They came twenty miles to meet him, and the principal chiefs, riding beside him, conducted him to the camp in great triumph. During his visit, which lasted three days, the principal chiefs, Black Moon and Sitting Bull, who had been strong adversaries of the whites for the last four years of the war, watched constantly over the safety of the missionary; they slept beside him at night, lest some Indian might seek to avenge upon his person the death of some kinsman killed by the whites.

9 In North Dakota, on the Missouri River.

10 *Cassock*—a long robe.

During the day time, multitudes of children flocked to his lodge, and the mothers brought him their new babies that he might lay his hands on them and bless them.

In the gathering of the Indians the head chiefs promised to put an end to the war. Sitting Bull declared that he had been the most mortal enemy of the whites, and had fought them by every means in his power. But now that Black-robe had come to utter the words of peace, he renounced warfare and would never again lift his hand against the whites.

. . . Whatever may be the result of the treaty which the commission has just concluded with the Sioux, we can never forget nor shall we ever cease to admire, the disinterested devotion of the Reverend Father DeSmet. At the age of sixty-eight years, he did not hesitate in the midst of the heat of summer, to undertake a long and perilous journey, across the burning plains, destitute of trees and even of grass. Having none but corrupted and unwholesome water, he was constantly exposed to scalping by Indians. And this he did without seeking either honors or remuneration of any sort. His only interest was to stop the shedding of blood and save, if it might be, some lives, and preserve some habitations to these children of the desert. To their spiritual and temporal welfare he has consecrated a long life of labor and concern.

Colleges and Universities on the Frontier

In the early nineteenth century, men such as John Mason Peck called on the churches to assume responsibility for education on the frontier. How well various church bodies responded to that challenge is indicated in part by the following list of colleges and universities established along or behind the advancing frontier.

Athens College (*Methodist*) 1842; Alabama, *north central*
Austin College (*Presbyterian*) 1849; Texas, *northeastern*
Baldwin-Wallace College (*Methodist*) 1845; Ohio, *northern*
Baylor University (*Baptist*) 1845; *east central*
Beloit College (*Congregational-Presbyterian*) 1846; Wisconsin, *south*
Bethany College (*Disciples of Christ*) 1840; West Virginia, *north*
Butler University (*Disciples of Christ*) 1850; Indiana, *central*
Capital University (*Lutheran*) 1850; Ohio, *central*

Carroll College (*Presbyterian*) 1846; Wisconsin, *southeast*
Carthage College (*Lutheran*) 1846; Illinois, *west*
Centenary College (*Methodist*) 1825; Louisiana, *northwest*
Clarke College (*Roman Catholic*) 1843; Iowa, *east*
Earlham College (*Quaker*) 1850; Indiana, *east*
Georgetown College (*Baptist*) 1829; Kentucky, *north central*
Grinnell College (*Congregational-Presbyterian*) 1846; Iowa, *central*
Hanover College (*Presbyterian*) 1827; Indiana, *southeast*
Heidelberg College (*German Reformed*) 1850; Ohio, *north*
Hiram College (*Disciples of Christ*) 1849; Ohio, *northeast*
Illinois College (*Congregational-Presbyterian*) 1829; Illinois, *west central*
Illinois Wesleyan (*Methodist*) 1850; Illinois, *central*
Iowa Wesleyan College (*Methodist*) 1842; Iowa, *east*
Kenyon College (*Episcopal*) 1826; Ohio, *central*
Lawrence College (*Methodist*) 1847; Wisconsin, *east central*
Lindenwood College (*Presbyterian*) 1827; Missouri, *east*
MacMurray College (*Methodist*) 1846; Illinois, *west central*
Marietta College (*Congregational*) 1830; Ohio, *southeast*
Mississippi College (*Baptist*) 1826; Mississippi, *southwest*
Mount Union College (*Methodist*) 1846; Ohio, *northeast*
Ohio Wesleyan College (*Methodist*) 1842; Ohio, *central*

States, territories, and cities: 1850

Olivet College (*Congregational*) 1844; Michigan, *south central*
Otterbein College (*United Brethren*) 1849; Ohio, *central*
Pacific University (*Congregational-Presbyterian*) 1849; Oregon, *northwest*
Rockford College (*Congregational-Presbyterian*) 1847; Illinois, *north*
St. Mary-of-the-Woods College (*Roman Catholic*) 1840; Indiana, *northeast*
St. Mary's College (*Roman Catholic*) 1844; Indiana, *north*
Shurtleff College (*Baptist*) 1827; Illinois, *southwest*
Southwestern College (*Methodist*) 1840; Texas, *central*
Southwestern at Memphis College (*Presbyterian*) 1848; Tennessee, *southwest*
Spring Hill College (*Roman Catholic*) 1836; Alabama, *southwest*
University of Dayton (*Roman Catholic*) 1850; Ohio, *southwest*
University of Indiana (*State*) 1830; Indiana, *south central*
University of Mississippi (*State*) 1844; Mississippi, *north*
University of Notre Dame (*Roman Catholic*) 1844; Indiana, *north*
Western Reserve University (*Congregational-Presbyterian*) 1826; Ohio, *north*
Willamette College (*Methodist*) 1842; Oregon, *northwest*
William Jewel College (*Baptist*) 1849; Missouri, *east central*
Wittenberg College (*Lutheran*) 1842; Ohio, *west*

1. Select those colleges founded between 1820 and 1830 and find their location on the map provided by your teacher.
   a. Where are most of these colleges located?
   b. How many are west of the Mississippi River?
   c. Who is establishing these colleges: governmental or denominational agencies?
2. Now find the location of colleges founded between 1840 and 1850.
   a. Where were most of the colleges established at this time?
   b. How many in this period are west of the Mississippi River?
   c. Which denominations are most active?
3. After plotting the colleges on the map, what generalizations could you make about the educational role of the churches compared to that of the state?

Town Meeting on the Frontier

The following paragraphs present the background for a short drama that you are to write.

Fort White is a booming frontier town. It sits on the edge of Indian territory and is barely three years old. A river town, Fort White is rapidly becoming a trading center. Furthermore, wagon trains taking settlers to California are now using Fort White as their jumping-off point. As a result of the new economic activity—horses, wagons, provisions for the settlers, etc.—the population of Fort White is rapidly growing. Also the *character* of the population is changing. Once the town seemed made up only of trappers, Indian traders, soldiers, ferryboat operators, saloonkeepers, and dance hall girls; now, storekeepers, craftsmen, farmers, and ranchers are bringing women and children to the area.

Recently some of the townspeople proposed that a church be invited to send a preacher out from the East. To make Fort White a more attractive place for a preacher and his family to settle, these townspeople also proposed putting up a church building and a parsonage. Some people received the idea with enthusiasm; some were skeptical or indifferent; a few were openly hostile.

Now a town meeting has been called. Everyone who has a strong feeling on the issue has crowded into the saloon to have a say. As you write your drama, be sure to include the thinking of a variety of people. A person may desire a church in town for a number of reasons or might oppose the church for various reasons. Some of the people you might have speak at the meeting are

buffalo hunters	doctors
soldiers	storekeepers
Indian scouts	horse traders
Indian leaders	ferryboat operators
saloonkeepers	farmers
housewives and mothers	bankers
gamblers	fur traders
lawyers	teachers

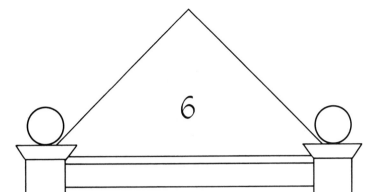

Black Americans
And The
Churches

INTRODUCTION

THE CHURCH AS
REFUGE AND HOPE

THE CHURCH DIVIDED
AND REPROACHED

CHRISTIANITY ABANDONED
AND CHRISTIANITY
CHALLENGED

Introduction

Spirituals and Their Message

Didn't My Lord Deliver Daniel?

Didn't My Lord deliver Daniel?
He delivered Daniel from the lion's den,
Jonah from the belly of the whale,
An' the Hebrew children from the fiery furnace,
An' why not every man?
Set my foot on the Gospel ship,
An' the ship begin to sail,
It landed me over on Canaan's shore
An' I'll never come back no more.

Run to Jesus

Run to Jesus, shun the danger,
I don't expect to stay much longer here.
He will be our dearest friend,
An' will help us to the end.
I don't expect to stay much longer here.

Oh Freedom!

Oh freedom! Oh freedom!
Oh freedom over me!
An' before I'd be a slave,
I'll be buried in my grave
An' go home to my Lord an' be free.

I Got Shoes

I got shoes, you got shoes,
All God's children got shoes.
When I get to heaven goin' to put on my shoes
I'm goin' to walk all over God's Heaven.
Heaven, Heaven.
Everybody talkin' 'bout Heaven ain't goin' there
Heaven, Heaven.
I'm goin' to walk all over God's Heaven.
[Other verses use *robe, harp,*
and *wings* in place of shoes.]

You Got a Right

You got a right, I got a right
We all got a right to the tree of life.
The very time I thought I was lost,
The dungeon shook an' the chain fell off.
You may hinder me here, but you cannot there,
'Cause God in Heaven goin' to answer prayer.

Inchin' Along

Keep a-inchin' along,
Keep a-inchin' along,
My Lord will come by'n bye;
Keep a-inchin' along, like a poor inch worm,
My Lord will come by'n bye.
'Twas a-inch by inch I sought the Lord,
An' a-inch by inch, He blessed by soul,
My Lord will come by'n bye.

Keep Your Hand on the Gospel Plow

Keep your hand on the Gospel plow,
Wouldn't take nothin' for my journey now, Holy Ghost
Keep your hand on the Gospel plow,
Hold on, Hold on,
Keep your hand on the Gospel plow,
Hold on.
Didn't come here for to stay always,
Just come here to fill my place.
I got a mother in the promised land,
Never shall rest till I shake her hand.

Slavery's Chain Done Broke at Last

Slavery's chain done broke at last
Goin' to praise God 'til I die.
I did know my Jesus heard me
'Cause the spirit spoke to me
An' said, "Rise my child, your children
An' you, too, shall be free."

Some of the preceding words as set to music have been most white Americans' only contact with the religion of black Americans. This distinctly Afro-American music has been enthusiastically adapted by white Americans for their own church choirs, pop singers, and even marching bands. In these new settings, however, the spiritual loses not only its original flavor but also its meaning. In original form the spiritual can provide insight into the role religion played and does play in the lives of many black Americans.

After you reread the lines of the spirituals and listen to recordings of some spirituals, try to answer the following:

1. What does each spiritual tell you about the things that mattered most to those who created them?
2. What do the subjects of the spirituals tell you about the conditions of the lives of those who sang them?
3. What are the central themes of the spirituals?
4. Do spirituals indicate the role of the church in the lives of black Americans?

As you read "Black Americans and the Churches" see if the information verifies your answers to the above questions.

Black Americans and Christianity

Most immigrants came to America because they wanted to. They hoped they would find across an ocean something better than the poverty or persecution or limited opportunity that most of them left behind. One large group of Americans, however, came as captives, as servants for life, as slaves. Not by choice but by force, they left a culture and civilization behind that could not be carried with them. It could not be transported because all tribal and even all family relationships were destroyed in the cruelties of the "middle passage" from Africa to the West Indies and in the countless cruelties that followed. The Negro arrived in America without a country. After three and one-half centuries of tragic exploitation, black Americans have not yet found a country.

Christianity was the slaveowners' religion. Yet black people embraced Christianity in large numbers. Those white Christians who thought of Christianity as *their* religion, *their* private possession, were amazed to learn that Christianity had not lost all of its early universality. Jesus had given clear expression to that universality in his command, "Go therefore and teach all nations . . ." (Matthew 28:19). That white clergymen in America did not with equal explicitness proclaim the universality of God's love was fully evident to the slave population. Some of the strongest words of reproach came from a free black man in Boston, David Walker (1785–1830), who called on members of the white church to repent while there was still time. In a powerful tract first published in 1829, *Appeal to the Coloured Citizens of the World*, Walker asked whether those words spoken by Jesus were really taken seriously in America.

> Can the American preachers appeal unto God, the Maker and Searcher of hearts, and tell Him, with the Bible in their hands, that they make no distinction on account of men's colour? Can they say, "O God! thou knowest all things—thou knowest that we make no distinction between thy creatures to whom we have to preach the Word"? Let them answer the Lord; and if they cannot do it in the affirmative, have they not departed from the Lord Jesus Christ, their master?[1]

Despite the refusal of most churches in nineteenth-century America to be color blind, black people in this country became Christians at a more rapid pace than did any other non-European people. Most became Baptists, with Methodists accounting for the next largest group. Smaller numbers became Presbyterians and Roman Catholics, with others scattered among a wide variety of denominations and sects. Today about two thirds of all black Americans have some church affiliation.

In the seventeenth and eighteenth centuries the slaves, without a trained clergy and without any financial resources, were obliged to attend the churches of their masters. Seating was usually, though not always, segregated; or services for whites and blacks were held at widely separated times on Sundays. As the total number of black church members grew, pressures for separate institutions for the two races increased. A particularly unhappy episode in Philadelphia in which black worshipers in the midst of services were abused and routed led to a decision to form a distinct church, free from such intolerable intervention. In 1787 Richard Allen, a former slave, withdrew from that city's Methodist church in order to gather all "Free Africans" into a church home of their own. Some decades later, similar organizations arose among the Baptists and Presbyterians. All of these became major vehicles for the expression of a powerful form of piety in America.

---

1 The text of Walker's *Appeal* may be found, among other places, in Herbert Aptheker (ed.), *One Continual Cry: David Walker's Appeal, Its Setting and Its Meaning* (New York: 1965), p. 107.

The Church
as Refuge and Hope

For the isolated and dispossessed black Americans—as for other disadvantaged and dispossessed in American history—the church became more than simply a place of worship. It was a social, educational, political, and recreational center. The doors to a professional career for the black man were all closed except one: the ministry. Thus black preachers occupied a central place in the life of the whole community. And the church could give identity and moral purpose to a disinherited race in need of both.

Among the many ways in which Christianity could sustain an oppressed people was to offer hope. Biblical religion was full of promise, portions of which were eagerly, desperately claimed. The Old Testament held out one kind of hope: escape from bondage. After all, didn't Moses deliver the Israelites from slavery in Egypt? Why then wouldn't God raise up a deliverer now to lead his black children out of their bondage? And so the words of the Negro spiritual were sung:

> *Go down Moses*
> *Way down in Egypt's land;*
> *Tell ole' Pharoah,*
> *"Let my people go."*

The New Testament held out another kind of hope: a better life in the world to come. "I am bound for the Promised Land." Life on this earth might be filled with suffering sorrow, might be marred by weeping and dying, but life on this earth was simply not the last word. Heaven awaits. There, God "will wipe away every tear from their eyes, and death shall be no more, neither shall there be mourning nor crying nor pain any more, for the former things have passed away" (Revelation 21:4).

After you have read the following two selections, be prepared to discuss these points:

1. The sermon of Richard Allen reflects both the attraction of Christianity for black slaves and the particular emphasis of black religion at this time.

   a. Why would this emphasis have special attraction in the 1830s and 1840s?

   b. Which spiritual does Allen's sermon most resemble? Be prepared to defend your choice.

2. E. Franklin Frazier states that the "pent-up emotions and frustrations" of the black people found an outlet in the church.

a. Why would the emotions of black people be "pent up"?

b. How might the church provide an outlet for these emotions?

3. Frazier also talks of black men and women achieving status in the church.

a. What is status?

b. How might one find status in a church? Explain.

c. Do you know men or women who today find "status" in their synagogues or churches? Have these people sought "status" for reasons similar to those of the nineteenth-century slave? Why or why not?

Students preparing for the ministry and other professions at Bethune-Cookman College, Daytona Beach, Florida, in 1943.

Richard Allen

Richard Allen (1760–1831), founder and first bishop of the African Methodist Episcopal Church, was a forceful preacher of earnest, effective piety. A former slave himself, he spoke in a sermon to his fellow sufferers of a better life beyond.

> I mention experience to you that your hearts may not sink at the discouraging prospects you may have, and that you may put your trust in God who sees your condition, and as a merciful father pitieth his children, so doth God pity them that love Him. . . . As life is short and uncertain, and the chief end of our being in this world is to be prepared for a better, I wish you to think of this more than anything else. Then you will have a view of that freedom which the sons of God enjoy. If the troubles of your condition end with your lives, you will be admitted to the freedom which God hath prepared for those of all colors that love him. Here the power of the most cruel master ends, and all sorrow and tears are wiped away.

E. Franklin Frazier

A modern black scholar, E. Franklin Frazier (1894–1962) told of the way in which the Negro church in America served as a refuge and a hope.[2]

> In providing a social life in which the Negro could give expression to his deepest feeling, and at the same time achieve status and find a meaningful existence, the Negro church provides a refuge in a hostile white world. For the slaves who worked and suffered in an alien world, religion offered an outlet for their pent-up emotions and frustrations. Moreover, it turned their minds from the sufferings of this world to a world after death where the weary would find rest and the victims of injustice would be compensated. The Negroes who were free before the Civil War found status in the church which shielded them from the contempt and discrimination of the white world. Then for a few brief years after Emancipation the hopes and expectations of the black freedmen were raised and they thought they would have acceptance and freedom in the white man's world. But their hopes and expectations were rudely shattered when white supremacy was re-established in the South.
>
> Where could the Negro find a refuge from this hostile white world? They remembered from their Bible that the friends of Job counseled him to curse God and die. They remembered too that Samson when blinded had torn down the Temple and destroyed himself along with his tormentors. . . . But the Negro masses did not curse God and die. They could not pull down the Temple upon the white man and themselves. They retained their faith in God and found a refuge in their churches.

The Church Divided
and Reproached

Early in the nineteenth century, all religious groups seemed to agree that slavery was an enormous evil. As an institution it stood condemned; men and governments were urged to get rid of it as quickly as possible. The Quakers in Philadelphia, for example, petitioned Congress in 1804 on behalf of the "African race." They urged especially that the slave trade itself be halted, that Congress put an end "to this dark and gloomy business"

---

2 From E. Franklin Frazier, *The Negro Church in America* (New York: Schocken Books, 1963). Copyright 1963 by the University of Liverpool. Reprinted with permission of Pantheon Books. See also Albert J. Raboteau, *Slave Religion* (New York: Oxford University Press, 1978).

as soon as it was constitutionally possible. In 1818, Presbyterians from both North and South gathered in their General Assembly to proclaim:

> We consider the voluntary enslaving of one part of the human race by another as a gross violation of the most precious and sacred rights of human nature; as utterly inconsistent with the law of God, which requires us to love our neighbor as ourselves; and as totally irreconcilable with the spirit and principles of the Gospel of Christ, which enjoin that "all things whatsoever ye would that men should do to you, do ye even so to them."

Nothing could appear more clear cut, more promising. The moral guidance of the churches was sure.

But then something happened. Around 1830, the sentiments began to shift, the words began to waver. As Northern abolitionists[3] grew more extreme, Southern apologists[4] grew more defensive. As slavery became less essential to the economy of the North, it was—with the invention of the cotton gin—becoming more essential in the South. As some attacked all slaveholders as evil, others attacked all those favoring emancipation as meddlers and false philosophers. Feelings on both sides hardened.

The growing division within the nation could be seen in the growing division within the churches. There, the disagreements were often more than just a matter of mere opinions. In some cases churches actually broke apart and denominations divided. Three major groups suffered such separations in the years before the Civil War: the Methodists (divided in 1844), the Baptists (divided in 1845), and the Presbyterians (divided in 1857). Of these three, only the Methodists and Presbyterians have reunited, the Methodists in 1939 and the Presbyterians in 1983. As Lincoln said in the dark days of the war, both sides "read the same Bible, and pray to the same God; and each invokes His aid against the other . . ." How could such a thing be?

1. After reading the following statements about the white churches and slavery, assemble the arguments both for and against slavery.
   a. Which points have a religious basis?
   b. Which points are nonreligious in nature?
2. Note the change in the Presbyterian position from 1818 to 1835. (Similar changes occurred in other churches.) What factors might account for this change?

3 *Abolitionists*—those seeking to do away with slavery completely; those wanting to abolish slavery everywhere at once were sometimes called *immediatists,* or radical abolitionists.

4 *Apologists*—the defenders of slavery and of slaveholding.

3. Some churches, such as the Quakers, never did alter their original position. Why?

Methodists

The division in Methodism is clearly seen in two statements. The first is the position taken by South Carolina's Methodist Bishop William Capers in 1836. The second statement consists of resolutions adopted by the Methodist Anti-slavery Convention meeting in Boston in 1843.

1.   We denounce the principles and opinions of the abolitionists in toto and do solemnly declare our conviction and belief that whether they were originated, as some business men have thought, as a money speculation or, as some politicians think, for electioneering purposes or, as we are inclined to believe, in a false philosophy, overreaching and setting aside the Scriptures through a vain conceit of a higher refinement, they are utterly erroneous and altogether hurtful.

2.   Resolved, that the holding or treating human beings as property, or claiming the right to hold or treat them as property, is a flagrant violation of the law of God; it is sin itself; a sin in the abstract and in the concrete; a sin under all circumstances, and in every person claiming such right, and no apology whatever can be admitted to justify the perpetration.
   Resolved, that as the unanimity and harmony of feeling which should ever characterize the people of God cannot exist so long as slavery continues in the Church, we feel it our imperative duty to use all such means as become Christians in seeking its immediate and entire abolition from the Church of which we are members.

Baptists

Contrasting Baptist sentiments are evident in the following paragraphs: the first, Richard Furman's *Exposition of the Views of the Baptists Relative to the Coloured Population* . . . (1823) and the second, John Mason Peck's *Journal* entry for the first days of 1842.

1.   While men remain in the chains of ignorance and error, and under the dominion of tyrant lusts and passions, they cannot be free. And the more freedom of action they have in this state, they are but the

more qualified by it to do injury, both to themselves and others. It is, therefore, firmly believed that general emancipation to the Negroes in this country would not, in present circumstances, be for their own happiness as a body, while it would be extremely injurious to the community at large in various ways.

2.   January 1, Nashville. Today I attended for a few moments a sale in the market-place. A negro boy was sold who appeared about twelve years old. He stood by the auctioneer on the market-bench with his hat off, crying and sobbing, his countenance a picture of woe. I know not the circumstances; but it was the first human being I ever saw set up for sale, and it filled me with indescribable emotions. Slavery in Tennessee is certainly not as oppressive, inhuman and depressing as the state of the poorer classes of society in England, Ireland, and many parts of Continental Europe; yet slavery in its best state is a violation of man's nature and of the Christian law of love.

Presbyterians

In the same newspaper (*New York Evangelist*) on the same day (November 21, 1835) Presbyterians in South Carolina differed sharply with Presbyterians in Michigan.

1.   Resolved, that in the opinion of this presbytery [Charleston Union], the holding of slaves, so far from being a sin in the sight of God, is nowhere condemned in his Holy Word—that it is in accordance with the example, or consistent with the precepts of patriarchs, prophets and apostles; and that it is compatible with the most fraternal regard to the best good of those servants whom God may have committed to our charge, and that, therefore, they who assume the contrary position, and lay it down as a fundamental principle in morals and religion, that all slaveholding is wrong, proceed upon false principles.

2.   Resolved, that this synod [of Michigan] believe the buying, selling and owning of slaves in this country to be A Sin Before God and man; that the system of American slavery is a great moral, political, physical and social evil, and ought to be immediately and universally abandoned—and that it is our duty, by the use of all kind and known means, and especially by cultivating a spirit of sympathy and prayer for the enslaved, and their masters, as well as of general moderation and wisdom in the dissemination of truth and light, to endeavor to hasten the happy day of universal emancipation.

From all of the above it would be easy to assume that the abolition or the continuance of slavery was a controversy chiefly or exclusively among the whites. But Negro abolitionists were also active and—to some—frighteningly effective. Walker's *Appeal*, noted above, provoked rage and denunciation among Southern legislatures and newspapers; it even worried many white abolitionists by what was regarded as its "bold, daring, inflammatory" nature. Others, however, and especially blacks themselves, were warmed and enheartened by the forceful, passionate call for freedom. Henry Highland Garnet (1815–1882), a black clergyman, newspaper editor, and United States Minister to Liberia, praised Walker's work as the first and "actually the boldest and most direct appeal in behalf of freedom." Walker, Garnet, and other blacks published newspapers, called conventions, issued tracts, petitioned legislatures, and in many other ways demonstrated that abolitionism was by no means exclusively a white man's movement. And the hostility which the black abolitionist aroused exceeded even that of his counterpart among the whites. ". . . his very presence on the antislavery platform challenged those popular notions which had stereotyped his people as passive, meek, and docile. As a common laborer, the Negro might be tolerated, even valued, for his services; as an anti-slavery agitator, he was frequently mobbed."[5]

Frederick Douglass

The most successful black abolitionist was Frederick Douglass. Born in Maryland in 1817, Douglass managed to escape to Massachusetts in 1838. In 1845 he wrote his autobiography, *Narrative of the Life of . . . An American Slave.* In an appendix to that work, he turned his attention to the white churches in America, and the word he spoke was one of rebuke and reproach.

As you read the selection from Frederick Douglass' autobiography keep in mind the following:

1. What church is Douglass opposed to? Why?
2. What does he mean by "partial" and "impartial" Christianity?
3. Why does Douglass use words such as *hypocritical, misnomer, fraud, libel*? How does he support use of these words?
4. Note that Douglass condemns that type of Christianity that is "in union with slaveholders." What evidence can you find that many Christians actively opposed slavery in this period?

5 Leon F. Litwack, *North of Slavery: The Negro in the Free States, 1790–1860* (Chicago: 1961), p. 231. See also Benjamin Quarles, *Black Abolitionists* (New York: Oxford University Press, 1969).

I have spoken in such a tone and manner, respecting religion, as may possibly lead those people unacquainted with my religious views to think me an opponent of all religion. To remove such misunderstanding, I give the following brief explanation. What I have said respecting and against religion, I mean strictly to apply to the *slaveholding religion* of this land, and with no possible reference to Christianity proper. For, between the Christianity of this land, and the Christianity of Christ, I recognize the widest possible difference—so wide, that to receive the one as good, pure, and holy, is of necessity to reject the other as bad, corrupt, and wicked. To be the friend of the one, is of necessity to be the enemy of the other. I love the pure, peaceable, and impartial Christianity of Christ. I therefore hate the corrupt, slaveholding, women-whipping, cradle-plundering, partial and hypocritical Christianity of this land. Indeed, I can see no reason, but the most deceitful one, for calling the religion of this land Christianity. I look upon it as the climax of all misnomers, the boldest of all frauds, and the grossest of all libels ... We have men-stealers for ministers, women-whippers for missionaries[6] and cradle-plunderers for church members. The man who wields the blood-clotted whip during the week fills the pulpit on Sunday, and claims to be a minister of the meek and lowly Jesus. The man who robs me of my earnings at the end of each week meets me as a class-leader on Sunday morning, to show me the way of life, and the path of salvation ... He who proclaims it a religious duty to read the Bible denies me the right of learning to read the name of the God who made me. He who is the religious advocate of marriage robs whole millions of its sacred influence, and leaves them to the ravages of wholesale pollution. The warm defender of the sacredness of the family relation is the same person that scatters whole families—separating husbands and wives, parents and children, sisters and brothers—leaving the hut vacant, and the hearth desolate. We have men sold to build churches, women sold to support the gospel, and babes sold to purchase Bibles for the *poor heathen! all for the glory of God and the good of souls!* The slave auctioneer's bell and the church-going bell chime in with each other, and the bitter cries of the heartbroken slave are drowned in the religious shouts of his pious master. Revivals of religion and revivals in the slave-trade go hand in hand together. The slave prison and the church stand near each other. The clanking of fetters and the rattling of chains in the prison, and the pious psalm and solemn prayer in the church, may be heard at the same time. The dealers in the bodies and souls of

---

6 *Missionary*—one sent by a church to proclaim the gospel to infidels; an evangelist, at home or abroad, especially the latter.

men erect their stand in the presence of the pulpit, and they mutually help each other. . . .

Such is, very briefly, my view of the religion of this land; and to avoid any misunderstanding, growing out of the use of general terms, I mean, by the religion of this land, that which is revealed in the words, deeds, and actions, of those bodies, north and south, calling themselves Christian churches, and yet in union with slaveholders. It is against religion, as presented by these bodies, that I have felt it my duty to testify.

Christianity Abandoned and Christianity Challenged

Twentieth-century Americans were beset by many problems. Some related to the rapid industrialization and automation of so many phases of life. Others stemmed from the great growth of the cities, with the population of urban centers mounting as the number of farm dwellers declined. There were also problems of war, of poverty, of labor and management, of health, hunger, and housing. Some Americans felt with peculiar force the burden of an added problem: namely, race.

Leading Denominations of Black Christians in America, 1980

	APPROXIMATE MEMBERSHIP IN MILLIONS
National Baptist Convention, Incorporated	6.3
Church of God in Christ (Pentecostal)	3.0
African Methodist Episcopal Church	2.25
African Methodist Episcopal Zion Church	1.3
National Baptist Convention, Unincorporated	1.0
Progressive National Baptist Convention	.75

A total of over fourteen million members may be found on the church rolls of these six denominations alone, though as scholar L. N. Jones has noted, "active membership must be well below this figure." See Milton C. Sernett, ed., *Afro-American Religious History: A Documentary Witness* (Durham, NC: Duke University Press, 1985), pp. 493-494.

In the critical area of civil rights, the black church was often the rallying point. It served in many capacities: as recruitment center, as assembly ground, as cafeteria and hotel, as morale booster, and as first-aid station. Unfortunately, it also served as the symbol of changing racial patterns for those who wished above all to preserve the status quo. Thus, black churches were bombed and burned and black clergymen were jailed or slain. In 1964, a Baptist church in Birmingham, Alabama, was bombed while Sunday school was being held; four black girls were killed.

The strong stand in behalf of civil rights taken by the black churches was seldom matched by the white churches. Though individual whites—young and old—marched, prayed, argued, and went to jail, the whole force of organized Christendom did not spend itself in a battle for "liberty and justice for all." Opinions were divided as they had been one hundred years before, though now both denominational and geographical lines were blurred.

One result of this renewed division was a repetition of the rebuke of Frederick Douglass. The churches had again lost an opportunity to be

A. Phillip Randolph, son of a Methodist minister and head of the Sleeping Car Porters Union, leads a demonstration at the Democratic National Convention in the 1940s. The demonstrators demanded an end to segregation in the military—and in all aspects of life in America.

A white supremacist group, the Ku Klux Klan, marched in the streets of St. Petersburg, Florida, about 1926.

loyal to "the Christianity of Christ." Some critics, however, went even farther. They not only saw the churches as failing to be loyal to their own heritage, but they saw Christianity as having failed also. For too many centuries, Christianity had been identified with the political power and personal ambitions of white men. Since it was a white man's religion, black men must turn elsewhere for spiritual guidance and support. So argued Malcolm Little (1925–1965), better known as Malcolm X.

Malcolm X

Starting in the 1930s, the Black Muslims represented as much a rejection of Christianity as they did a dedication to the Islamic faith. Malcolm X turned from traditional Christianity to a life of crime and indulgence, then to a new and changed life as a Black Muslim preacher. He was in the process of still another transition when he was assassinated on February 21, 1965. His *Autobiography,* which was nearing completion when he died, tells of his abandonment of Christianity for Islam.

As you read this brief section of the *Autobiography of Malcolm X,*[7] keep in mind the following:

1. What has Christianity done to the black man, according to Malcolm X?
2. What reasons can you infer for his leaving Christianity?
3. Is there anything in Malcolm X's writing that indicates it was written in the 1960s rather than in the 1850s? If so, what?

Human history's greatest crime was the traffic in black flesh when the devil white man went into Africa and murdered and kidnapped to bring to the West in chains, in slave ships, millions of black men, women, and children, who were worked and beaten and tortured as slaves.

7 Excerpts from "Satan" from *The Autobiography of Malcolm X.* Reprinted with permission of Grove Press, Inc. Copyright ©1964 by Alex Haley and Malcolm X. Copyright ©1965 by Alex Haley and Betty Shabazz. Also by permission of Hutchison Publishing Group, Ltd.

The devil white man cut these black people off from all knowledge of their own kind, and cut them off from any knowledge of their own language, religion, and past culture, until the black man in America was the earth's only race of people who had absolutely no knowledge of his true identity. . . .

This "Negro" was taught of his native Africa that it was peopled by heathen, black savages, swinging like monkeys from trees. This "Negro" accepted this along with every other teaching of the slavemaster that was designed to make him accept and obey and worship the white man.

And where the religion of every other people on earth taught its believers of a God with whom

In 1964 Martin Luther King, Jr., and Malcolm X greeted each other in Washington, D.C. One year later, Malcolm X was assassinated; three years after that King, too, was assassinated.

they could identify, a God who at least looked like one of their own kind, the slavemaster injected his Christian religion into this "Negro." This "Negro" was taught to worship an alien God having the same blond hair, pale skin, and blue eyes as the slavemaster.

This religion taught the "Negro" that black was a curse. It taught him to hate everything black, including himself. It taught him that everything white was good, to be admired, respected, and loved. It brainwashed this "Negro" to think he was superior if his complexion showed more of the white pollution of the slavemaster. This white man's Christian religion further deceived and brainwashed this "Negro" to always turn the other cheek, and grin, and scrape, and bow, and be humble, and to sing, and to pray, and to take whatever was dished out by the devilish white man; and to look for his pie in the sky, and for his heaven in the hereafter, while right here on earth the slavemaster white man enjoyed *his* heaven.

Martin Luther King, Jr.

As indicated earlier in this study, much of the civil rights movement had its focus in the black churches. To a great degree, this broad participation was made possible and effective through the patient, imaginative leadership of Martin Luther King, Jr. (1929–1968). That leadership also prevented Christianity from becoming altogether a white man's religion. In King, the churches found themselves being challenged instead of rejected; some were inspired and some were threatened, but none was ignored.

A Baptist minister and a child of the South, King became pastor in 1954 of the Dexter Avenue Baptist Church in Montgomery, Alabama. There he first came into national prominence as the leader of a bus boycott that lasted 381 days. Before it was over, patterns of segregated

In September of 1988, Barbara Harris of Philadelphia made history when she became the first woman bishop in the 200-year history of the Episcopal Church.

seating at lunch counters, in theatres, and other public places—in addition to buses—were vastly altered. The most dramatic moment in Dr. King's leadership of the civil rights movement came in the nonviolent march that he led to the nation's capital in August, 1963. A portion of his stirring address on that occasion is given below. On April 4, 1968, King was, like Malcolm X, struck down by an assassin's bullet. Also like Malcolm X, he was not yet forty years of age when death so brutally and abruptly came.

As you read the following portion of Martin Luther King's speech,[8] keep in mind the following questions:

1. What challenge does Dr. King throw out to the churches?
2. How does Dr. King (as compared with Richard Allen) see his role as a clergyman?

There will be neither rest nor tranquility in America until the Negro is granted his citizenship rights. The whirlwinds of revolt will continue to shake the foundations of our nation until the bright day of justice emerges . . .

Continue to work with the faith that honor in suffering is redemptive. Go back to Mississippi, go back to Alabama, go back to Louisiana, go back to the slums and ghettos of our Northern cities, knowing that

---

8 Reprinted by permission of Joan Daves. Copyright ©1963 by Martin Luther King, Jr.

somehow this situation can and will be changed.

Even though we face the difficulties of today and tomorrow, I still have a dream . . .

I have a dream that one day this nation will rise up and live out the true meaning of its creed: "We hold these truths to be self-evident, that all men are created equal."

I have a dream that one day on the red hills of Georgia the sons of former slaves and the sons of former slave-owners will be able to sit down together at the table of brotherhood.

I have a dream that one day even the state of Mississippi, a state sweltering with the heat of people's injustice, sweltering with the heat of oppression, will be transformed into an oasis of freedom and justice.

I have a dream that my four little children will one day live in a nation where they will not be judged by the color of their skin but by the content of their character.

I have a dream that one day every valley shall be exalted, every hill and mountain shall be made low, the rough places will be made plain, and the crooked places will be made straight, and the glory of the Lord shall be revealed and all flesh shall see it together. . . .

This will be the day when all of God's children will be able to sing with new meaning:

> My Country, 'Tis of Thee
> Sweet land of liberty
> Of Thee I sing.
> Land where my fathers died,
> Land of the pilgrims' pride
> From every mountainside
> Let freedom ring.

So let freedom ring. . . . When we let it ring from every village and every hamlet, from every state and every city, we will speed up that day when all of God's children, black men and white men, Jews and Gentiles, Protestants and Catholics, will be able to join hands and sing in the words of the old Negro spiritual:

> Free at last! Free at last!
> Thank God Almighty! We're free at last!

7

Religion: Personal and Social

INTRODUCTION

PERSONAL RELIGION

HASIDISM:
RELIGION — PERSONAL
AND SOCIAL

SOCIAL RELIGION

ORGANIZED RELIGION
AND AMERICAN SOCIETY

MIDDLETOWN:
A CASE FOR PANEL
DISCUSSION

Introduction

In American history, religion has exercised its force in two distinctive ways. It has been a force in *personal* behavior, in changing the minds, hearts, and lives of individuals. This might be regarded as the psychological dimension of religion. It has been a force in the *social* order, in affecting or altering social, economic, and political structures. This might be regarded as the sociological aspect of religion.

While these two kinds of activity can be distinguished from each other, they are not necessarily opposed to or even separated from each other. That is, a force that changes attitudes may also as a consequence produce changes in political behavior—perhaps even in politics itself. The reverse may equally be true. That is, a force that rearranges the social order may end up by also rearranging personal patterns of life and thought. It should be clear, therefore, that a personal approach to religion and a social approach need not be contradictory to each other. They may, in fact, support and aid each other.

Nevertheless, in the nation's development, there have often been periods—and persons—that have emphasized or preferred one aspect of religion more than the other. Some have seen the business of religion as primarily that of changing people's hearts and bringing about a right relationship with God, both here and hereafter. Others have seen the major task of religion as dealing with such social questions as war and peace, capital and labor, prejudice and poverty, and the like. In looking at the two broad areas in which religion does operate, you will want to decide what the strengths and weaknesses are in both realms. What does personal religion achieve? What should it achieve? Similarly, what does social religion do, and what should it seek to do?

Personal Religion

Revivalism

Popular and famous revivalists have been an outstanding feature in American history. Often their fame was such as to make them almost as well known abroad as they were in their own country. From George Whitefield in the eighteenth century to Billy Graham in the twentieth century, revivals have been a familiar part of American life.

What is a revival? Usually, it is a series of religious services held within a period of a few days or weeks that raises interest and excitement above the normal level. It revives the dull and tired spirits of church members or of passive Christians. It also recruits, brings into the church those previously not identified with it. The process during which people turn to God is generally called *conversion* and "making converts" has been considered a major function of most revivals.

As you read the selections of the revivalists, keep in mind the following:

1. What did the conversion experience do for Finney? What do you, from this account, consider to be the nature of the conversion experience?
2. Would you consider Moody's understanding of the nature of conversion to be the same as Finney's? Why or why not?
3. In what ways are the themes of Moody and Graham similar?
4. Judging from the selection by Billy Graham, what characteristics of the modern person (and society) need changing?
5. According to Graham, why can't a great society be realized without conversion?

Charles G. Finney

In the first half of the nineteenth century, the most famous American leader of revivals was Charles G. Finney (1792–1875). In addition to being a revivalist, he was a pastor, a professor, and a college president (Oberlin in Ohio). Before all this, he had prepared for a career in law. He also delivered lectures on how to promote and conduct revivals, being convinced that God used this "new measure" to "*wake up* a slumbering church." In his autobiography (published in 1876), Finney describes his own conversion experience. From this account, we can get some idea of why Finney would treat conversion as a most significant experience. We can also understand why he would expect others to have a similar sudden shift in their lives.

Conversion to Christ[1]

On a Sabbath[2] evening in the autumn of 1821, I made up my mind that I would settle the question of my soul's salvation[3] at once. If it

1 From *Memoirs of Rev. Charles G. Finney,* (New York, 1876), Chapter 2; the language has been slightly modified.

2 *Sabbath*—the seventh day of the Jewish week: i.e., Saturday. By extension, the term has been applied to the first day of the Christian week: i.e., Sunday.

3 *Salvation*—in a Christian context, the state of complete liberation from sin, of wholeness and oneness with God.

were possible, I would make my peace with God. I resolved as far as possible to avoid all business, and to give myself wholly to the work of securing the salvation of my soul. I was, however, obliged to be a good deal in the [law] office. But as the providence of God would have it, I was not very busy either on Monday or Tuesday. I had an opportunity to read my Bible and engage in prayer most of the time.

. . . During Monday and Tuesday my concern increased. Still it seemed as if my heart grew harder. I could not shed a tear; I could not pray. I avoided, as much as I could, speaking to anybody on any subject. Tuesday night I became very nervous. In the night a strange feeling came over me, as if I was about to die. I knew that if I did I should sink down to hell, but I quieted myself as best I could until morning.

At an early hour I started for the office. But just before I arrived something seemed to confront me with questions like these. Indeed, it seemed as if the inquiry was within myself, as if an inward voice said to me, "What are you waiting for? Did you not promise to give your heart to God? Now what are you trying to do? Are you trying to establish a righteousness all of your own?"

Just at this point the whole question of Gospel[4] salvation came to me in a most marvelous manner. I think I saw then, as clearly as I ever have in my life, the reality and fullness of the sacrifice of Christ. I saw that His work was a finished work. I saw that instead of having or needing any righteousness of my own to recommend me to God, I only had to submit myself to the righteousness of God through Christ. Gospel salvation seemed to me to be an offer of something to be accepted. It was full and complete. All that was necessary on my part was to get my own consent to give up my sins and accept Christ. Salvation, instead of being a thing to be worked out by me, was a thing to be found entirely in the Lord Jesus Christ.

Without being distinctly aware of it I had stopped in the street right where the inward voice seemed to halt me. How long I remained in that position I cannot say. But after a minute another question seemed to be put, "Will you accept it now, today?" I replied, "Yes, I will accept today, or I will die in the attempt."

Instead of going to the office, I turned and bent my course toward the woods, feeling that I must be alone and away from all human eyes and ears, so that I could pour out my prayer to God. . . . [After much despair, prayer, and inward struggle and after several hours had passed] it seemed as if I met the Lord Jesus Christ face to face. It did not occur

4 Gospel—literally, "good news" or "glad tidings"; the teachings of Jesus and the early apostles; any of the books Matthew, Mark, Luke, John, detailing the life and teaching of Jesus.

to me then, nor did it for some time afterward, that it was wholly a mental state. On the contrary it seemed to me that I saw him as I would any other man. . . .

I must have continued in this state for a good while. But my mind was too much absorbed to remember anything that was said. But I know that I received a mighty baptism of the Holy Ghost. Without any expectation of it, without ever having the thought that there was any such thing for me, without ever remembering that I had ever heard the thing mentioned by any person in the world, the Holy Spirit descended upon me in a manner that seemed to go through me, body and soul. I could feel the impression like a wave of electricity, going through and through me. It seemed like the very breath of God.

Dwight L. Moody

In the second half of the nineteenth century, Dwight L. Moody's name was most often associated with the successes of mass evangelism.[5] Like Finney, Moody (1837–1899) did not start out to be a minister. Once turned toward that profession, however, Moody—also like Finney— gave it all his energy and talent. With many prominent and wealthy supporters in America and abroad, Moody made an impact in several areas of national life. His preaching style was quiet and restrained, and his sermons—as the following excerpt reveals—were homey and easy to understand. This sermon was delivered in New York City in the spring of 1876 during a series of services that lasted fifty days.

Famous revivalist, Dwight L. Moody, shown in New York City's Hippodrome about 1876.

Ye Must Be Born Again[6]

I will direct your attention to the third chapter of John and the third verse: "Jesus answered and said unto him, Verily, verily, I say unto thee,

5 *Evangelism*—seeking religious converts with conspicuous effort and zeal.

6 From M.L. Simons (ed.), *Holding the Fort: Comprising Sermons and Addresses at the Great Revival Meetings. . . .* (Philadelphia, 1877), pp. 81-82.

except a man be born again, he cannot see the kingdom of God." You will see by the third chapter of Romans that it is absolutely necessary that a man be born again. You see in the third chapter of Romans what man is by nature. If you want to find out what God is, turn to the third chapter of John: "God so loved the world that He gave His only begotten Son, that whosoever believes in Him shall have everlasting life." Yes, read the third chapter of Romans if you want to find out how man lost life. Then read the third chapter of John, and read it prayerfully and with God's Spirit in you, and you will see how man is going to get everlasting life back again. I don't know a chapter that ought to be read more in a Christian spirit and read more deeply than that chapter. It is so plain and reasonable.

If there are a thousand people here tonight who want to know what love God has for them, let them read the third chapter of John and they will find it there, and find eternal life. They need not go out of this hall tonight to find eternal life. They will find it here in this chapter, and find eternal life before these services close. They hear tonight how the way for salvation of their souls is open to them. Yes, I do not know anything more important than this subject of regeneration [being born again]. I don't know of anything in the Bible more important and more plain than that, and yet it is a question that neither the church nor the world is sound upon. There is no question upon which the church and the world are more confounded than upon this very question of regeneration. If a man is sound on every other subject, you will find that he is unsound on this plain subject of regeneration. It is the very foundation of our hope, and the very foundation of our religion. It is a great deal better, with God's help, to understand this question perfectly first, then to go on further in the world of God. It is a solemn question—"Am I born of the Spirit? Have I been born again?" For you know that "Except a man be born again he cannot see the kingdom of God."

Billy Graham

In the twentieth century many Americans believed that mass evangelism had outlived its usefulness or effectiveness. They argued that the revival technique was more appropriate to the frontier period of American history, to the time when most people lived in the hamlets (instead of the large cities) and worked on the small farms (instead of in the huge factories). Other Americans, however, argued just the opposite. The large cities, they said, increased the opportunity for the revivalist to reach great

Evangelist Billy Graham is shown here "working the crowd" with former President Richard Nixon in Pittsburg, Pennsylvania, in 1968.

numbers of people. Also, advances in the techniques of communication—notably radio and television—increased the size of the audiences in marvelous, almost magical ways. The man who gave strongest support to this second position was Dr. William F. Graham (1918—), much better known as Billy Graham. Like Moody, he also proved very effective in crusades abroad. Unlike Moody, he was able to take advantage of modern technology and rapid transportation to reach thousands, even millions. Following is a portion of a 1965 sermon.

The Kingdom Society[7]

In our century various American Presidents have provided slogans to dramatize their philosophies of government. President Harding gave us "Back to Normalcy"; President Franklin Roosevelt, the "New Deal"; President Truman, the "Fair Deal"; President Kennedy, the "New

7 From *The Kingdom Society,* by Billy Graham. Reprinted from September, 1965 *Decision* magazine, copyright 1965 Billy Graham Evangelistic Association. Used by permission.

Frontier"; and President Johnson has set out for us the "Great Society." Jesus Christ of Nazareth also used slogans in his ministry. For example, he said, "Blessed are the poor in spirit: for theirs is the kingdom of heaven" (Matthew 5:3). It was one of many slogans that he used to announce his own "great society," which is the kingdom. . . .

How does the Kingdom Society differ from the other societies that men are devising today?

First, conversion is a requirement of citizenship. The kingdoms of this world do not require a change in human nature. Any religious belief will do; the philosophy of this world is, "It doesn't matter what you believe, just so you are sincere." But Jesus Christ said, "Except ye be converted . . . ye shall not enter into the kingdom of heaven" (Matthew 18:3). The world says that the only requirement is that we be reasonably decent and respectable. To be a member of the Kingdom of God there must be an inner change.

The story has been told many times, but still bears repeating. A Communist speaking in London's Hyde Park pointed to a pitiful tramp and said, "Communism will put a new suit on that man." A Christian standing in the crowd replied, "Yes, but Jesus Christ will put a new man in that suit!" In the Kingdom Society men are transformed from the inside out by the power of God.

The Kingdom Society will endure because it is comprised of men who have enduring character. "[God] hath delivered us from the power of darkness, and hath translated us into the kingdom of his dear Son: in whom we have redemption through his blood, even the forgiveness of sins," wrote the Apostle Paul to the Colossians (1:13-14). God demands a righteousness which is apart from the law and apart from our own efforts.

Fallible men cannot create an infallible society, but redeemed men can redeem society. You cannot produce a superior social order with men who hate, connive, take advantage, pillage and swindle, with self-interest as the motivation. National greed and selfishness are the corporate expressions of self-interest, which Jesus predicted would still exist in the last agonizing days of man's history.

He said, "For nation shall rise against nation, and kingdom against kingdom. . . . And then shall many be offended, and shall betray one another, and shall hate one another" (Matthew 24:7,10). This self-interest must be eliminated by the transforming power of Christ if we are to be part of the Kingdom Society. And Jesus made it a [command] when he said to Nicodemus, "Except a man be born again, he cannot see the kingdom of God" (John 3:3). Yes, conversion is a requirement for membership in the Kingdom Society that Jesus talked about.

Second the Kingdom Society is built upon love rather than hate. The way of the world is hate and tyranny and chaos.

. . . But in the Kingdom Society love is the dominant ethic. . . .

Third, the Kingdom Society is not built on the profit motive. The verb of the world is "get." The verb of the Christian is "give". . . .

How do you get into the Kingdom Society? Jesus said: "You must be born again" (John 3:7). "Not of blood, nor of the will of the flesh, nor of the will of man, but of God" (John 1:13). And, "As many as received him, to them gave he power to become the sons of God, even to them that believe on his name" (John 1:12).

Christ is saying to those who are on the outside, "Him that cometh to me I will in no wise cast out" (John 6:37). His hand, his heart, is extended to all who will repent of their sins and accept him as Savior.

"What if I don't?" you ask. The alternative is fearful. "He that believeth in him is not condemned: But he that believeth not is condemned already" (John 3:18). "He that hath the Son hath life; and he that hath not the Son of God hath not life" (1 John 5:12). "And many of them that sleep in the dust of the earth shall awake, some to everlasting life, and some to *shame and everlasting contempt*," said Daniel (12:2).

Social orders have come and gone. That is what was wrong with them—they were transient. But you may become a member of the Kingdom Society—the Kingdom of the redeemed. God is our Father; Jesus Christ is our elder Brother; the Holy Spirit is our abiding Comforter, Guide and Teacher; and the devil is no relation at all. Today you may join the "aristocracy" of heaven. You may become a legal son of God through Jesus Christ. And I bear this news to you upon the authority and under the seal of the King himself.

Receive Christ as your Savior. Be converted today and join the Kingdom Society. March under the flag of Jesus Christ. Sing his song. Commit your life to him, and find fulfillment in Jesus Christ!

New Institutions: The Salvation Army

Those who favored a personal rather than a social religion did not necessarily ignore the material or the physical. One who ministered to the individual could still minister to the *whole* individual. So it would be misleading and unfair to think of personal religion only in terms of private meditation or salvation of souls. Attention was in fact given to the basic necessities of food, clothing, and shelter. Concern was also expressed for needs almost as basic as those just named: recreation, vocational training, medical care, education, moral development, and the like.

Evangeline Booth, field commissioner (and later general) for the Salvation Army, is shown here about the beginning of World War I.

Dislocations caused by leaving the farm for the city seemed to work special hardships on young people. Away from the protection and familiar ways of family and friends, they often found the city a frightening and lonely place. The same was true of young people newly arrived in America from European villages and farms. They were even farther from the familiar security that they had previously known.

Many new organizations, therefore, came into being that were specifically aimed at meeting the needs of youth. The Young Men's and Young Women's Christian Associations became important institutions in America in the post-Civil War period. The Y saw to it that homeless were housed, that the jobless were employed, and that the bored and lonely were entertained. The game of basketball was invented by a YMCA official as a way to help pass the long winter hours when outdoor sports were impossible.

In a similar fashion, the Young Men's and Young Women's Hebrew Associations helped young people face the challenges of an urban and industrial life—young people who had little experience in either. For them all the problems of adjustment were added to the hardships of immigration; Jewish boys and girls had to learn a new language, understand a different society, and help fashion an adopted country. Later the YMHA and the YWHA developed the Jewish Community Centers where social, cultural, and religious needs were met for young and old alike.

The Catholic Young Men's National Union, formed in 1875, carried out many of the same sorts of tasks already described. Wholesome recreation was provided, night-school education was offered, religious counseling and strengthening was available. Other Roman Catholic organizations that were especially effective in meeting individual needs for young and old include the Knights of Columbus, founded in America in 1882; the Catholic Youth Organization, founded in Chicago in 1930; and the Society of St. Vincent de Paul, which originated in France but began its work in this country in 1845. The Society of St. Vincent de Paul was seeking, of course, to prevent the tragedies and misfortunes that awaited young men and young women. But when tragedy did come, the Society then was ready to offer even more of its material and spiritual support.

One new institution that may be considered representative of the many that took seriously their responsibilities for the *whole* individual is the Salvation Army, organized in England by William and Catherine Booth in 1865. Coming to the United States in 1879, this novel Army soon won wide respect for its obvious devotion to simple goodwill. The sick were visited, the hungry were fed, the poor were clothed. Before the days of welfare agencies and enlarged governmental responsibilities, the Salvation Army provided shelter and comfort that could be found nowhere else.

As you read about the Salvation Army, keep in mind the following:

1. What type of "ministering" does the Salvation Army engage in?
2. Does this make it different from other churches? If so, how?
3. What justification is there for saying the Salvation Army is representative of personal rather than social religion?

Sallie Chesham

In 1965, Sallie Chesham's official history of the Salvation Army was published: *Born to Battle: The Salvation Army in America*. Containing a friendly foreword from Dwight D. Eisenhower, the book tells the story of the Army from an insider's point of view. The following excerpt is taken from the Preface.

Born to Battle[8]

Most people today are aware of the Salvation Army. Fewer, perhaps, are familiar with its beliefs, objectives, or the extent of its services. As an international religious and charitable movement organized on a semi-military pattern, the Army is unique. The motivation for this organization, as with all churches, is love for God and a practical concern for the needs of humanity, expressed by a spiritual ministry. But no other church seeks the particular outreach the Army does, judging every member a fighting soldier; no other church has such a variety of bastions, from homes for unmarried mothers to mobile canteens. The Army has been called a "church-plus," "a religious organization with a social aim and a social organization with a religious aim," and "a force for God," but possibly the "militant arm of the Christian Church" fits best.

From the first day of his evangelistic ministry, founder William Booth was consumed by social concern. "You can't preach to a man on an empty stomach," he explained, and proceeded to open the first Army shelter home. As he observed the squalor of living conditions in London, the brutal treatment of children, and the growth of white slavery, programs and solutions evolved. Nevertheless, from the very first, he made this point: "Our primary responsibility is not to take man out of the slums, but to take the slums out of man." The Army has built on that premise for 100 years.

"No other man is General of an army of people that circles the globe," stated the *Chicago Interocean* of William Booth in 1903. "No other man is called commander by men and women of so many nationalities." This applies even more today [1963], for the Army serves in 69 countries, and is heard in 162 languages and dialects. It has 16,767 corps and outposts, 25,418 officers and 117,227 local officers or lay leaders. It operates 490 homes for the homeless, 205 men's work centers, 29 general hospitals, 12 convalescent hospitals, 86 maternity homes for unwed mothers, 6 leprosaria[9], 72 dispensaries and clinics, 13 probation and training homes, and 121 fresh air camps.

Additionally, it supplies leadership, education, bible, and music training to thousands of young people and adults, and operates children's homes, community centers, boys' and girls' clubs, golden-age centers, correctional services, and employment bureaus. Its family ser-

---

8 From Sallie Chesham, *Born to Battle*, copyright 1965 by The Salvation Army. Published by Rand McNally & Company. Reprinted with permission from The Salvation Army.

9 *Leprosaria*—institutions for the care of people afflicted with leprosy.

vice departments supply both emergency and long-term aid, its members and friends visit various institutions regularly, operate emergency and disaster service mobile canteens and hospitality centers for service personnel.

William Booth never wanted nominal members. He wanted active soldiers. The Salvationist is a combatant against sin, deprivation, sorrow, and illness. He feels compelled by God to live for others. He declares his belief that the Army was raised up by God and is sustained by him, and he affirms his acceptance of Army rules and regulations and Army tenets of doctrine.[10]

Joan Moss

In 1967, Joan Moss, a senior at San Francisco State College and a member of the Salvation Army, went to South America. There she worked in some of the Army's institutions—particularly in a leper colony in Paraguay. In *War Cry*, the official organ of Salvationists in the United States, she tells of her experiences along with some of her reflections on them.

A Man Cannot Live By Bread Alone[11]

I must tell you—though it hurts my pride—that during my first few days in Asuncion, Paraguay, I sort of cried myself to sleep. It was very cold. The living accommodation was not quite like that at home. The food was different. In a sense I felt alone and wondered if I had made a mistake—and then I really became involved.

My specific assignment was to work with some 50 young people ranging in age from 4 to 17. Some had been abandoned by their parents; some had been sent to the institution because the parents could not support them; some had been committed by the state. It was then that I suddenly realized that I had a commitment, and that as I worked with these young people my uniform in itself communicated a promise—"Here is help; here is happiness; here is love."

Suddenly hours meant nothing to me. The cold weather, the deprivations with which I had to live, the loneliness, passed away as if by magic. I came to know Maria and Irma and Pedro and Adelberta as though they really belonged to me.

10 *Doctrine*—literally, "teaching"; in religion, a teaching that has some official or formal status.

11 *The War Cry*, March 22, 1969, Vol. 89, No. 12, pp. 3, 6.

When I went to my own room some of the children would make any excuse to come in and see me. Mostly they were silly little things like, "I have a sore arm"—but the arm *wasn't* sore; or, "I cut my foot"—but I could find no cut; or, "I want to talk to you"—but I could tell they were making up a story; and suddenly it dawned on me that they loved me, and I loved them. There was a togetherness, a genuine love.

During my stay in South America, the United States news magazines and the local newspapers, presidential commissions and economists were all giving their versions of the race riots, ghetto living, civil disorders and multiple urban problems back home. I sincerely believe that every American should honestly examine himself and his attitudes in these vital areas. As members of the Salvationist Service Corps we did expose ourselves to the actual conditions of life. We did involve ourselves in an effort to help the people help themselves. The cost for me personally was much more than dollars and cents; I gained an understanding of people as I really shared myself with them. . . .

May there come to each of us a revelation of our part in the alleviation of hate among men. May there come to all of us an overwhelming urge to love and give of ourselves and, more important, to live Christ—for man cannot live by bread alone.

Hasidism: Religion—Personal and Social

Revivalism and the Salvation Army do not, of course, exhaust the examples of personal religion in America. Many other possibilities might be cited, such as the Quaker Inner Light, the monk's contemplative life in Roman Catholicism, the search for self-realization in a variety of contexts.

A particularly interesting example of personal religion that is also social is found within Judaism. An eighteenth-century pietistic movement known as Hasidism found its way to this country in the twentieth century, settling in and around Brooklyn, New York. Originating in Europe, the Hasidic groups often migrated *as communities*, keeping intact their special combination of intensely personal piety and clearly social community.

Martin Buber (1878–1965) is the best known interpreter of Hasidism, having "carried it into the world against its will," as he has said. He believed that this powerful religious movement should be carried into the world in order to remind modern man of the purposes for which he has been placed on earth. And this is what Hasidism is all about: the purpose of

12 Reprinted from *Hasidism and Modern Man* by Martin Buber, by permission of the publisher Horizon Press, New York, copyright 1958.

life. The selection below is adapted from Buber's *Hasidism and Modern Man.*[12] As you read this passage, consider the following questions.

1. What element is common to all movements that may be called Hasidic?
2. What do you think Buber means by "soul-force"?
3. From Buber's brief summary, what aspects of Hasidism seem mainly personal?
4. How useful or important is it in Hasidism to distinguish between the personal and the social?

The Hebrew word *Hasid* means "a pious man." There have again been communities in post-exilic[13] Judaism that bore the name Hasidim, the pious. . . . What is common to all of them is that they wanted to take seriously their piety, their relation to the divine in earthly life. They did not content themselves with the preaching of divine teaching and the practice of divine rituals, but sought to erect men's life-together on the foundation of divine truth. This is especially clear in the last-named community, [founded around the middle of the eighteenth century]. . . .

Martin Buber explained how the Hasidic movement had meaning in modern society.

Nowhere in the last centuries has the soul-force of Judaism so manifested itself as in Hasidism. The old power lives in it that once held the immortal fast to earth, as Jacob the angel, in order that it might fulfill itself in mortal life. But at the same time a new freedom announces itself therein. Without an iota being altered in the law, in the ritual, in the traditional life-norms, the long-accustomed arose in a fresh light and meaning. Still bound to the medieval in its outward appearance, Hasidic Judaism is already open to renewal in its inner truth.

This is not the place to present the teachings of Hasidism. They can be summed up in a single sentence: God can be beheld in each thing and reached through each pure deed. . . . In the Hasidic teaching,

13 After the exile into Babylonia in the sixth century before the rise of Christianity.

the whole world is only a word out of the mouth of God. Nonetheless, the least thing in the world is worthy that through it God should reveal Himself to the man who truly seeks Him; for no thing can exist without a divine spark. Each person can uncover and redeem this spark at each time and through each action, even the most ordinary, if only he performs it in purity, wholly directed to God and concentrated in Him. Therefore, it will not do to serve God only in isolated hours and with set words and gestures. One must serve God with one's whole life, with the whole of the everyday, with the whole of reality. The salvation of man does not lie in his holding himself far removed from the worldly, but in consecrating it to holy, the divine meaning: his work and his food, his rest and his wandering, the structure of the family and the structure of society. It lies in his preserving the great love of God for all creatures, yes, for all things. Hasidism took the social form of a great popular community—not an order of the secluded, not a brotherhood of the select, but a popular community in all its medley, in all its spiritual and social multiplicity. Never yet in Europe has such a community thus established the whole of life as a unity on the basis of the inwardly known. Here is no separation between faith and work, between truth and verification, or, in the language of today, between morality and politics; here all is one kingdom, one spirit, one reality.

Social Religion

In American Protestantism, the emphasis on applying Christianity to economic, social, and political structures received the tag of "social gospel." In Roman Catholicism, Christianity so applied was often spoken of as "social action." And in Judaism, a term frequently employed in treating these same concerns was "social justice." In all cases, the intent was similar: namely, to make ancient religious heritages relevant to modern social problems. To those standing in the Judeo-Christian tradition, this approach appeared to have very respectable precedents. For the Hebrew prophets had repeatedly condemned injustice centuries before the beginning of the Christian era. Eight centuries before the appearance of Christianity, for example, the prophet Amos had declared:

> *Hear this, you who trample upon the needy,*
> *and bring the poor of the land to an end,*
> *saying, "When will the new moon be over,*
> *that we may sell grain?*

And the sabbath,
  that we may offer wheat for sale,
  that we may make the ephah small and the shekel great,
  and deal deceitfully with false balances . . ."
AMOS 8:4-5

The essence of the prophet's message was briefly this:

> *Hate evil and love good,*
>   *and establish justice in the gate.* (5:18)

The Social Gospel

Among the first major advocates in America for a "social gospel" was Washington Gladden (1836–1918). A pastor in Columbus, Ohio, Gladden came to know firsthand the problems created by the big city and the big factory. No longer was it enough, he argued, to talk only of "changing men's hearts." One must also change their heads—and their environment. The very titles of Gladden's books reveal his emphasis and interest: *Applied Christianity* (1889) and *Social Salvation* (1902). The selection following, taken from *Applied Christianity*, deals specifically with the employer-employee relationship.

As you read the excerpt by the Reverend Washington Gladden, keep in mind the following:

1. How is Gladden's attitude similar to that of the prophet Amos, as expressed above?
2. What is Gladden's feeling toward regeneration? How does this compare with Moody's attitude?
3. What must the churches do in addition to changing people's hearts? Why, in your opinion, does Gladden take this position?

The Wage-Workers and the Churches[14]

. . . When a man is converted, he has a purpose to do right; and if you choose to go a little farther and say that he has the disposition to do right, I will not stop to dispute you. But he may have very crude ideas as to what right is; his heart may be regenerated, but his head may

---

14 Washington Gladden. *Applied Christianity* (Boston: 1889), pp. 170-173.

still be sadly muddled. And there are thousands of people in all our churches who mean to do right by their working people, but whose ideas have been so perverted by a false political economy that they are continually doing them grievous wrong. . . .

All good Christians believe, of course, that they ought to love their neighbors as themselves; but there are many among them who need help in answering the question, "Who is my neighbor?" The idea that the operatives in his factory, the brakemen on his freight trains, the miners in his coal mines are his neighbors, is an idea that does not come home to many a good Christian. He has been told that the law that governs his relations with them—the only law that can usefully govern his relations with them—is the law of competition, the law of supply and demand. In all this vast industrial realm, as he has been taught, self-interest is the only motive power. In the family, in social life, to a certain extent also in civil life, the force of good-will must be combined with the force of self-love. But in the industrial world, in the relations of employer and employed, this benevolent impulse must be suppressed. In this kingdom of industry they say that good-will is an intruder. In the family, in the neighborhood, in the state, if men were governed only by self-interest, we should have endless strife. In the industrial world, if we are governed by self-interest alone, we shall have peace and plenty. So the good Christian has been instructed. Over the entrance to the thronging avenues and the humming workshops of the industrial realm, an unmoral science has written, in iron letters: "ALL LOVE ABANDON, YE WHO ENTER HERE!" If beyond those portals is pandemonium, who can wonder? The first business of the Church of God is to preach that legend down, and to put in place of it: "YOUR WAGE-WORKER IS YOUR NEAREST NEIGHBOR."

Social Justice

In the twentieth century, a strong and steady voice repeatedly raised on behalf of social justice was that of Rabbi Stephen S. Wise (1874–1949). Involved in humanitarian efforts along a wide front, Wise fought economic oppression, political corruption, social indifference, international brutality, and every form of intolerance or bigotry. Among the founders of the National Association for the Advancement of Colored People, Wise also helped bring into being the American Jewish Congress, which has worked for justice and equality for all Americans. Two selections adapted from his autobiography follow. The first shows his conviction that religion be made relevant to the world in which we live. The second, occasioned by a factory fire in New York City in which many young women employees were burned to death, shows concerns comparable to those of Gladden. As you read the selections by Rabbi Wise, keep in mind the following:

1. What does Wise mean by a "minister going into politics"? What is his attitude toward this?
2. Wise quotes from the Hebrew Bible: "Justice, Justice shalt thou pursue." What do you think this means to Wise?
3. Concerning social justice and social equality, what must the churches and synagogues generally do? What might they specifically do?
4. Why might the churches and synagogues be "forces of respectability and convention" rather than "forces of righteousness"? Is Rabbi Wise, in your opinion, being fair to the churches and synagogues? Why or why not?

Pulpit and Politics[15]

Shall a minister, ought a minister go into politics? What are the reasons that make it unwise for a minister to go into politics? I have heard them given over and over again: "Politics and religion have nothing to do with each other; for the minister to go into politics leads to divisiveness; religion should deal with general principles and not their daily applications; the minister in politics is apt to go off into partisanship as he did in the work of the Anti-Saloon League and during the days of Prohibition fanaticism." The maxim of Jesus, "Render unto Caesar," was repeated over and over again to enforce this position, and too often it was joined in spirit with the phrase, "The poor ye have always with you."

I felt very early in my ministry the necessity and advantages of the minister going into politics. To me neither religion nor politics was remote from life. Religion is a vision or ideal of life. Politics is a method of life. To say that the minister should not go into politics is to imply that ideal and reality are separate and alien. Politics is what it is because religion keeps out of it.

I am persuaded that the minister can go into politics without partisanship, without compromise. And most important, he must seek nothing for himself or his church, and accept nothing. Convinced that the ideals of religion, separated from their day-to-day application, were

15 Stephen S. Wise. *Challenging Years*. Reprinted by permission of G. P. Putnam's Sons. Copyright ©1949 by G. P. Putnam's Sons.

meaningless, I early entered into one area of controversy after another that many might call political, and which I recognized as part of the social and political life of America. There were many state, national, and international issues in which I felt that as a minister of religion I had a place.

Throughout my life it seemed to me that all ministers of religion were for justice in principle, but too ready to be silent about injustice in practice. One of the dangers of all of us is that we are willing to fight for justice for ourselves alone, forgetting that justice will be for all or none. For me the supreme declaration of our Hebrew Bible was and remains: "Justice, Justice shalt thou pursue"—whether it be easy or hard, whether it be justice to white or black, Jew or Christian.

A Rabbi Sides with Labor

If the church and the synagogue were forces of righteousness in the world instead of being the forces of respectability and convention, this thing [the tragic fire] need not have been. If it be the shame and humiliation of the whole community, it is double the humiliation of the synagogue and of the church which have suffered it to come to pass. We may not be ready to prescribe a legislative program nor devise an industrial cure, but we must demand and demand unceasingly an ever-increasing measure of social equity and social justice.

The hour has come for industrial peace. It must be peace with honor,—say some. But it must be more than peace with honor. It must be peace with security as well. We would have no peace with honor for some, and, at the same time, deny security to all. The issue at stake is not the open shop but the closed door, which shuts out the toilers from safety and justice.

The lesson of the hour is that while property is good, life is better, that while possessions are valuable, life is priceless. The meaning of the hour is that the life of the lowliest worker in the nation is sacred and inviolable, and, if that sacred human right be violated, we shall stand adjudged and condemned before the tribunal of God and of history.

Social Action

Monsignor John A. Ryan (1869–1945) led America's Roman Catholic community to increased levels of awareness and commitment regarding

In 1972 the first female rabbi was ordained in the United States.

society's ills. A professor of "Moral Theology and Industrial Ethics" at the Catholic University of America in Washington, D.C., Ryan later moved into administrative positions where his impact was even more direct. Under his prodding, a Department of Social Action came into being as a major unit of the National Catholic Welfare Conference. Ryan was also a prolific author, writing such books as *Social Reconstruction, A Living Wage,* and *Social Doctrine in Action.* In *Social Reconstruction* (published in 1920), Ryan concluded with some comments about the "Bishops' Program" adopted the year before; you will find out more about that program later in this lesson.

As you read the selection by Father Ryan, keep in mind the following:

1. What philosophy had developed in America that Ryan and the Bishops agreed was false?
2. What particular social issue therefore drew the attention of these clergymen?
3. What seem to be the objections to the Bishops' Program? Who is doing the objecting?

The Bishops' Program[16]

Are these proposals of the Bishops' Program, taken as a whole or any of them, what might be called radical? Well, some persons think so, including some Catholics. A friend of mine—a priest—told me not long ago that some person stated in his hearing, "We are willing to listen to the Bishops when they talk to us about going to Mass on Sunday, or approaching the Sacraments, or any other of our religious duties; but when they go into the field of business and industry, as they have done in this Program, we do not feel obliged to follow them." Had there been something in the Program to the effect that labor unions were unqualifiedly bad and to be condemned and shunned, I fancy that the man who was talking to my friend would have applauded that quite as much as if it were purely a religious pronouncement. The persons who regard this Program as radical are basing their opinions not on Catholic principles, but upon an exaggerated notion of the rights of private property.

The notion of property fostered by the capitalist system, and the privileges and opportunities that have been accorded to property in that system, are excessive. The rights of property are not unlimited. There is nothing in Catholic doctrine to support any such theory. Open any Catholic manual of moral philosophy or moral theology, and you will find the statement that the primary right of property is the right of *use,* not the right of ownership. God made the earth for all the children of men. The primary destination and purpose of the goods of this world is to support human beings, to support human life, and that means the human life of all. There is nothing in nature—or in revelation—to indicate that any class of persons has a prior claim over another class to the goods of the earth. The primary right of property is, therefore, the right of access to the goods of the earth.

The right of private property, the right of the individual to exclude others from a particular portion of the goods of the earth, is always held subject to the general, primary right of use and access which belongs to all human beings. That is what we mean by saying that the right of property is not unlimited, that it is not absolute. That is what we mean, that is what the Bishops' Program means, when it declares that wealth is stewardship, that the owner of any particular piece of private property is not the absolute owner of it, but a trustee under God. Being a trustee or steward, he is bound to use the goods that he

16 John A. Ryan. *Social Reconstruction* (New York: MacMillan Co., 1920), pp. 208-209.

calls his in such a way as to comply with the fundamental purpose of all natural goods.

Organized Religion and American Society

The institutions of religion—America's churches and synagogues—gradually responded to the challenge put forward by Gladden, Wise, Ryan, and many others. Particularly with the onslaught of World War I and the intensified social problems that war always brings, the cultural application of religious values and insights seemed more urgent than ever.

The three official statements presented below, given in order of their proclamation, reveal the intimate involvement of major religious institutions with major social issues. Note the points of comparison among them. Do these social questions have a Protestant, a Jewish, and a Catholic answer that is distinctive? Or do they all have answers within a broader system of values and human concerns?

As you read the statements of the three religious organizations, keep in mind the following:

1. What similarities exist in the three programs? What differences? Does "social religion" have distinctive denominational emphasis or not? Support your answer.
2. How much of the programs presented here has become reality?
3. Which of the goals have yet to be attained?
4. What might account for the realization of some but not of other goals?
5. Are there any goals that you feel are not appropriate or desirable? If so, which ones and why? Are there goals here that you think are not the business of organized religion? If so, which ones, and why?

A Social Creed of the Churches[17]

(1) We deem it the duty of all Christian people to concern themselves directly with certain practical industrial problems. To us it seems that churches must stand:

For equal rights and complete justice for all men in all stations of life.

For the rights of all men to the opportunity for self-maintenance,

17 Adopted in 1908 by the (Protestant) Federal Council of Churches (later, the National Council of Churches).

a right ever to be wisely and strongly safeguarded against encroach-ments of every kind. For the right of workers to some protection against the hardships often resulting from the swift crises of industrial change.

For the principle of conciliation and arbitration in industrial dissentions.

For the protection of the worker from dangerous machinery, occu-pational disease, injuries and mortality.

For the abolition of child labor.

For such regulation of the conditions of toil for women as shall safeguard the physical and moral health of the community.

For the suppression of the "sweating system" [working under the most adverse conditions, e.g., factories in tenement homes].

For the gradual and reasonable reduction of the hours of labor to the lowest practicable point, and for that degree of leisure for all which is a condition of the highest human life.

For a release from employment one day in seven.

For a living wage as a minimum in every industry, and for the highest wage that each industry can afford.

For the most equitable division of the products of industry that can ultimately be devised.

For suitable provision for the old age of the workers and for those incapacitated by injury.

For the abatement of poverty.

A Statement[18]

1. A more equitable distribution of the profits of industry.
2. A minimum wage which will insure for all workers a fair standard of living.
3. The legal enactment of an eight hour day as a maximum for all industrial workers.
4. A compulsory one-day-of-rest-in-seven for all workers.
5. Regulation of industrial conditions to give all workers a safe and sanitary working environment, with particular reference to the special needs of women.
6. Abolition of child labor and raising the standard of age wherever the legal age limit is lower than is consistent with moral and physical health.
7. Adequate workmen's compensation for industrial accidents and occupational diseases.

18 Adopted by the Central Conference of American Rabbis, 1918.

Children of Italian agricultural workers are cared for and instructed by the Home Missions Council of North America.

8. Legislative provision for universal workmen's health insurance and careful study of social insurance methods for meeting the contingencies of unemployment and old age.

9. An adequate, permanent national system of public employment bureaus to make possible the proper distribution of the labor forces of America.

10. Recognition of the right of labor to organize and to bargain collectively.

11. The application of the principles of mediation, conciliation and arbitration to industrial disputes.

12. Proper housing for working-people, secured through government regulation when necessary.

13. The preservation and integrity of the home by a system of mother's pensions.

14. Constructive care of dependents, defectives and criminals, with the aim of restoring them to normal life wherever possible.

Bishops' Program of Social Reconstruction[19]

"Society," said Pope Leo XIII, "can be healed in no other way than by a return to Christian life and Christian institutions." The truth of these

19 Epilogue adopted in 1919 by the National Catholic War Council (later, the National Catholic Welfare Conference; now, the United States Catholic Conference).

words is more widely perceived today than when they were written, more than twenty-seven years ago. Changes in our economic and political systems will have only partial and feeble efficiency if they be not reinforced by the Christian view of work and wealth. Neither the moderate reforms advocated in this paper nor any other program of betterment or reconstruction will prove reasonably effective without a reform in the spirit of both labor and capital. The laborer must come to realize that he owes his employer and society an honest day's work in return for a fair wage, and that conditions cannot be substantially improved until he roots out the desire to get a maximum of return for a minimum of service. The capitalist must likewise get a new viewpoint. He needs to learn the long-forgotten truth that wealth is stewardship, that profit-making is not the basic justification of business enterprise, and that there are such things as fair profits, fair interest, and fair prices. Above and before all, he must cultivate and strengthen within his mind the truth which many of his class have begun to grasp for the first time during the present war; namely, that the laborer is a human being, not merely an instrument of production; and that the laborer's right to a decent livelihood is the first moral charge upon industry. . . . This is the human and Christian, in contrast to the purely commercial and pagan, ethics of industry.

Middletown:
A Case for a Panel Discussion

Middletown was once a prosperous commercial center. Fifty years ago it was the hub of rail transportation in the state. However, with the elimination of passenger service and a decline in freight hauling, the great rail yards with their huge locomotive shops are now little used. The factory, which once turned out railroad cars by the thousands and operated two eight-hour shifts a day, is now producing at one-third capacity. Many men are out of work. Others managed to find only part-time employment. For some the hardship proved too great and they deserted their wives and children. A large number of families were forced to go on welfare. Middletown seemed to be dying on the vine.

Recent editions of the newspaper tell yet another story. Robberies and burglaries have increased sharply. An editorial warned of a local alcoholism problem as arrests for public drunkenness increase in number. Parents are particularly concerned about a recent wave of juvenile delinquency. Middletown is becoming no place to live.

Attempts to bring new industries to Middletown have been in vain. Unfavorable tax and zoning laws, a poor school system, and charges of corruption in local government have made Middletown unattractive to businessmen searching for places to locate. Machine politics have also effectively thwarted reform. Middletown seems unable or unwilling to help itself.

One evening a group of thirty clergymen gather to explore possible courses of action that they and their churches might undertake to meet the pressing problems facing Middletown's citizens. Five clergymen form a panel to present their thinking to the group. Reactions to the panel's presentation are invited. In this discussion a wide variety of philosophies are revealed and subsequently a number of proposals are offered.

Assignment: Reconstruct that panel discussion. The panel members represent a variety of religious traditions and offer options consistent with their tradition. The panel consists of the following. The personal orientations are reflected in the readings noted in parentheses.

Dr. Robert Brown: Baptist (Billy Graham, Moody, etc.)
Captain Catherine Smith: the Salvation Army (the Salvation Army, YWCA, etc.)
Father Patrick Murphy: Catholic (Ryan, Social Action)
Rabbi David Cohen: Jewish (Wise, Social Justice)
Moderator: secretary of the Middletown Council of Churches

8

Ways of Understanding: Science and Religion

APPROACHES TO NATURE

SCIENCE AND RELIGION
AT WAR

CHRISTIANS DISAGREE
ON DARWIN

DARWIN, THE COURTS,
AND THE SCHOOLS

THE BIBLE AND EVOLUTION

CREATIONISM
AND THE CLASSROOM

Approaches to Nature

If someone says the word *nature,* what do you think of first? Do you think of sunsets, mountains, and rivers? Or do you think of telescopes, microscopes, and atomic weight tables? What is your basic approach to nature? Do you ask first of all, "How can I enjoy it?" Or do you ask, "How can I control it?" Or perhaps you ask, "How can I escape it?"

These questions are intended only to suggest that there are different attitudes, different goals, even different languages. And it is not always especially helpful to say that one approach is right and another approach is wrong. What we can do is discover the merits or strengths of the differing approaches.

Consider these two comments on familiar objects of our environment:

> *When I look at thy heavens, the work*
> *of thy fingers,*
> *the moon and the stars which thou*
> *hast established;*
> *What is man that thou are mindful of him*
> *and the son of man that thou dost care*
> *for him?*   —PSALMS 8:3,4

A quite rudimentary study of the general facts known about the stars is sufficient to show that they are objects of the same general character as the Sun. That is to say, each is an effectively independent body held together by its own gravitation and [giving off heat] from its own resources. . . . It turns out, indeed, that the Sun is a "pretty average" star in almost every respect.   —W.H. McCREA, *Physics of the Sun and Stars* (London: Hutchinson's University Library, 1950), p. 106.

Now, these are quite different sorts of statements. Some of the differences are obvious to you immediately. For example, because of the way the lines are arranged, you suspect that one is poetry—even if it doesn't rhyme—and the other is prose. There are other differences, too: of perception, of interests, of language. You may want to list the differences that you can find between the two passages.

Having noted the differences, is it really very helpful to ask which statement is true, or which one is right and which one is wrong? Actually, as you have probably guessed by now, that is not the real point. Rather, we are interested in seeing the variety of ways in which people deal with the world of nature. Some fear it, some sing about it, some may worship it, and some may investigate or analyze it. Also, there are those who work to preserve and conserve the natural surroundings while others may exploit or destroy them.

Science and Religion At War

Many of the arguments between science and religion arise from these differences in viewpoint and interest. Where one group is more powerful politically than the other, then the arguments may become bitter battles. At the end of the nineteenth century, scholar Andrew D. White even wrote *A History of the Warfare of Science with Theology in Christendom*.[1] But the "warfare" is by no means limited to Christianity—or to America.

The Western world has experienced science-religion arguments about earthquakes and lightning rods, about eclipses and meteorites, about epidemics and vaccination, about the age of rocks and the shape of the earth. In America, the greatest controversy was created by Darwin's research and writing on evolution. He published in 1859 the *Origin of Species*, which raised the basic question, whether one species over a long period of time could evolve into a quite different species. In 1871, his *Descent of Man* raised questions about the human species in connection with "natural selection" over a time span of many hundreds of thousands of years.

So a large number of scientific questions were posed. How old is the earth? How did life on earth begin? What brings about changes from lower forms of life to higher? How many species were originally "created"? What forces create change? Are these forces within man's control or not?

It is clear that these questions are more than scientific inquiries. Religious and philosophical issues or concerns are also involved. Furthermore, the evolution controversy was not a case in which all scientists were on one side and all theologians on the other. Some able scientists found Darwin's arguments convincing, but others did not. Some noted clergymen saw evolution as a threat to the Christian religion, while others understood evolution as "God's way of doing things." With so many important questions being raised and with so many contrasting responses to these questions, it is no surprise that the theories about evolution have caused a long and intense controversy. For a hundred years the loud and sometimes angry words of debate have been heard.

---

1 Available in paperbound edition from Dover (2 vols.) and Free Press. See also David C. Lindberg and Ronald L. Numbers, *God and Nature: Historical Essays on the Encounter Between Christianity and Science* (Berkeley, Calif.: University of California Press, 1986).

Christians Disagree on Darwin

Only three years after Darwin published his *Descent of Man* (1871), a professor at Princeton Seminary in New Jersey responded. Charles Hodge (1797–1878) in *What is Darwinism?* pointed out some difficulties that this scientific theory created for Christian teaching or doctrine. Hodge was especially concerned about what seemed to be the denial of design or intelligence in the plan of nature. What, then, was the role of the Creator?

At the same time, in the 1870s, Lyman Abbott (1835–1922) was beginning to argue in favor of evolution

Lyman Abbott, one of the defenders of the theory of evolution, in 1905.

as a support of Christian teaching. Darwin's theories showed how human beings could gradually emerge "from an animal nature into a spiritual manhood." A pastor of the Plymouth Congregational Church in Brooklyn, Abbott even wrote a book entitled *The Theology of an Evolutionist* (1897). For him, evolution was more than merely neutral with regard to religious convictions. It was, or could be, a positive aid.

As you read the selections by each of these men, keep in mind the following:

1. For Hodge, what was the evidence that there is design in nature?
2. What are the consequences of a denial of design in nature?
3. What effect did the theory of evolution have on Abbott's belief?
4. What was Abbott's main reason for believing evolution to be true?

Charles Hodge

What Is Darwinism?[2]

All the many varieties of plants, all the countless forms of animals, all the varieties of men have been evolved, according to Darwin, by the

---

2 Charles Hodge. *What is Darwinism?* New York: Scribner, Armstrong & Co., 1874. Abridged and adapted.

blind, unconscious laws of nature. The grand and fatal objection to Darwinism is this exclusion of design in the origin of species. By design I mean the intelligent and voluntary selection of an end. I also mean the intelligent and voluntary choice, application and control necessary to accomplish that end.

Design therefore implies intelligence in its very nature. No man denies that this adaptation of means to a preconceived end is the work of the mind. Darwin does not deny it. No Darwinian denies it. What they do deny is that there is any design in nature. "It is merely apparent," they say. In thus denying design in nature, the Darwinians set themselves against the intuitions and convictions of all mankind—a barrier which no man has ever been able to surmount. Overpowering proof of intelligence and benevolent design lie all around us. If perplexities ever turn us away from them for a time, they come back upon us with irresistible force. Again and again we see that all living beings depend upon one everacting Creator and Ruler.

It is impossible for even Mr. Darwin to deny all design in the constitution of nature. What is his law of heredity? Why should like beget like? Take two germ cells, one of a plant, another of an animal; no man by microscope or by chemical analysis, or by the magic power of the spectroscope, can detect the slightest difference between them, yet the one infallibly develops into a plant and the other into an animal. Take the germ of a fish and a bird and they are equally indistinguishable; yet the one always under all conditions develops into a fish and the other into a bird. Why is this? There is no physical force, whether light, heat, electricity, or anything else, which makes the slightest approximation to accounting for that fact. . . .

The conclusion of the whole matter is that the denial of design in nature is virtually the denial of God. Mr. Darwin's theory does deny all design in nature, therefore, his theory is virtually atheistical;[3] his theory, not he himself. He believes in a Creator. But when that Creator, millions on millions of ages ago, did something—called matter and a living germ into existence—and then abandoned the universe to itself to be controlled by chance and necessity, without any purpose on His part as to the result, or any intervention or guidance, then He is virtually consigned, so far as we are concerned, to nonexistence.

3 *Atheistic*—characterized by atheism: the belief that there is no God.

Lyman Abbott

A Religious Revolution[4]

... Darwin's volume "The Descent of Man," published in 1871, had put before the world his conclusion that man is descended or, as I prefer to say, ascended from a prior animal race—a conclusion involving not only the origin of the race and the scientific accuracy of the Bible, but the origin, reality, and nature of sin and of its cure.

The current theory which had been almost universally accepted in the church for centuries, except in some minor details, may be briefly stated thus: God made man about six thousand years ago; made him innocent and virtuous. Man broke God's law, and as a result, his descendants inherited a depraved nature—that is, a tendency to sin. The world was therefore a kind of vast reformatory, populated solely by men and women possessed by evil predispositions. To suffer the penalty of their sins and make pardon and a mended career possible, Jesus Christ had come into the world. . . .

I believe that I am open-minded; my critics would say too open-minded. There is no theory which concerns the well-being of humanity which I am not willing to investigate . . . The doctrine of evolution, as expounded by Darwin, I found accepted by a steadily increasing number of scientific men. I recognized that they were as honest as I, as eager to learn the truth, and much more intelligent that I was upon all scientific subjects. I set myself to the task of getting a sympathetic acquaintance with their point of view and seeing what was its bearing on Christian faith. For the latter purpose I went back of the Christian creeds to the Bible. . . .

I was not long in coming to the conclusion that animal man was developed from a lower order of creation. This was the view of the scientific experts, and on questions on which I have no first-hand knowledge I accept the conclusions of those who have. Such scientific objections as the failure to discover a "missing link" I left the scientists to wrestle with. The objection that evolution could not be reconciled with Genesis gave me no concern, for I had long decided that the Bible is no authority on scientific questions. To the sneer, "So you think your ancestor was a monkey, do you!" I replied, "I would as soon have a monkey as a mud man for an ancestor." This sentence, first uttered, I believe, in a commencement address before the Northwestern University in Chicago, brought upon me an avalanche of condemnation—but no reply. In truth, no reply was possible. For the question whether God

4 Adapted from Lyman Abbott *Reminiscences*. Boston: Houghton Mifflin & Co., 1915.

made the animal man by a mechanical process in an hour or by a process of growth continuing through centuries is quite immaterial to one who believes that into man God breathes a divine life. . . . I accepted to the full John Fiske's[5] aphorism: "Evolution is God's way of doing things."

This doctrine of evolution not only tallied with the conclusions I had previously reached respecting the authority of the Bible, but clarified it. If evolution is God's way of doing other things, why not God's way of giving to mankind a revelation of himself and his will?

Darwin, The Courts, and the Schools

The lectures and addresses by Hodge and Abbott found echoes in a great many churches and synagogues in the closing years of the nineteenth century. Men debated, resisted, modified, and struggled as Darwinism came to America. The controversy was more, however, than just a matter of debate and discussion. Churches were broken up, professors were tried for heresy, and even entire denominations threatened to come apart.

The contest finally spread beyond the religious organizations to the courts and the schools. There the drama was at its height. One of the most famous trials in America's history took place in the hot summer of 1925 in Dayton, Tennessee. There a young high school biology teacher, John Scopes (1901–1970), was charged with violating a Tennessee law that read as follows:

Be it enacted by the general assembly of the State of Tennessee that it shall be unlawful for any teacher in any of the universities, normals[6] and all other public schools of the State, which are supported in whole or in part by the public school funds of the State, to teach any theory which denies the story of the Divine creation of man as taught in the Bible, and to teach instead that man has descended from a lower order of animals.

Young Scopes had as his defending attorney a famous Chicago lawyer, Clarence Darrow (1857–1938). The prosecuting attorney, William Jennings Bryan (1860–1925), was even more famous, for he had run for the office of President of the United States three times. With persons so well known and with an issue so highly controversial, the trial attracted nation-

5 John Fiske (1842–1901) was a popular philosopher and historian in America.

6 *Normals*—schools for training teachers.

wide attention. Reporters came from Baltimore, Chicago, and New York. Experts in biblical studies or biological sciences arrived from the East Coast and the West. The stage was set.[7] Dayton, Tennessee, a sleepy country town, was about to become famous all across the land.

Much of the tension was supplied by the two giant contenders, Darrow and Bryan. It sometimes seemed as though the young high school teacher was forgotten in all the excitement and shouting. Darrow even had Bryan himself put in the witness chair. The following exchange between the two lawyers is typical of the sharp language that echoed in that Tennessee courtroom.

Darrow:	*Do you believe Joshua made the sun stand still?*
Bryan:	*If the Bible says so, yes.*
Darrow:	*What would happen to the earth if the sun stood still?*
Bryan:	*I've never thought about it.*
Darrow:	*Don't you know it would have converted into a molten mass of matter?*
Bryan:	*You can testify to that when you get on the stand.*
Darrow:	*You have never investigated the subject?*
Bryan:	*I don't think I have ever had the question asked.*
Darrow:	*Or ever thought of it?*
Bryan:	*I have been too busy on things that I thought were of more importance than that.*
	(Then later in the day)
Bryan:	*I want the world to know that this man, who does not believe in a God, is trying to use a court in Tennessee to slur at the Bible.*
Darrow:	*I object to your statement. I am examining you on your fool ideas that no intelligent Christian on earth believes.*
The Judge:	*Court is adjourned until nine o'clock tomorrow morning.*

The trial lasted for twelve hot days, neither side budging the other side very far from its fundamental outlook on science and religion, on nature and the universe. When it was all over, the jury returned a verdict of guilty. The judge imposed a fine of $100 on the high school teacher, John Scopes. Scopes stood before the judge and said:

> Your honor, I feel that I have been convicted for violation of an unjust law. I will continue in the future, as I have in the past, to oppose this

---

7 The Scopes trial had enough drama to inspire an award-winning play, *Inherit the Wind*, by Jerome Lawrence and R.E. Lee (Bantam, 1960). You might enjoy reading it.

The War Against Evolution

By MIRIAM ALLEN DE FORD

HE physical strength of a healthy ape is three times
that of a human being, and the mental strength three
that of an evolutionist." Thus the *Golden Age*,
ous spokesman of Pastor Russell. And the Rever-
Bulgin, of Indianapolis, is even less complimentary:
is a bigger sin than murder or horse-stealing."
nt business man splutters to a scientific society:
y may be very good for monkeys and microbes,
en and women,"
oils of South-
re in Kansas
ged to state
eir study of
not under-
in God.
alist atti-
ns to be
condi-
spread
icism
east,
so-
ne
e

cases definitely reported to me where young people wen*
Christian homes to college, high schools, or universitie
came home evolutionists and atheists; therefore by it
shall it be known.

My work is for everybody that believes in
Creator and that the Bible is His revealed will
I am working for every boy and girl in Californi
they be Catholic, Protestant, or Jew, against
theory or hypothesis for an established fact
not right to tea
person. . . . To
camouflaged u
of science o
search is a f
ceptive cour
no conflict
and true r
a terrible
Bible a
. . . Wl
be com
suppo
own
shat'
des'
lai
ti
f

> The nation-wide drive against the teaching of evo-
> lution breaks out in newspaper dispatches day after
> day. Here is one day's grist:
>
> ### ARREST EVOLUTION TEACHER
>
> #### Tennessee Authorities Start Test
> #### Case Under New Law
>
> NASHVILLE, Tenn., May 6 (A. P.).—
> A Dayton, Tenn., dispatch to the *Ban-
> ner* says that J. T. Scopes, science
> teacher in Rhea High School, was ar-
> rested yesterday on a charge of violat-
> ing the new Tennessee law prohibiting
> the teaching of evolution in the State
> public schools.
>
> TALLAHASSEE, Fla., May 6.—Teach-
> ing evolution in the schools of Florida
> would be unlawful under provisions of
> a bill introduced in the House today.
> Any teacher found guilty of violating
> the provisions of the act would be dis-
> qualified to teach in the schools of
> Florida.

"GIT OUT AND STAY OUT"
—Rollin Kirby in the St. Louis *Post-Dispatch*.

*No teaching of evolution
for public school students
in selected areas in 1925.*

law in any way I can. Any other action would be in violation of my ideal of academic freedom.[8]

John Scopes, however, did not have to pay the $100. The case was appealed to the state supreme court where, on a technicality, the fine was set aside.

The central legal question at stake—whether Tennessee's law was unjust or not—did not reach the U.S. Supreme Court in the 1920s. In fact, not until 1968 did the highest court give its opinion. Then it responded to a similar law in Arkansas. The Court declared the "anti-evolution law" to be unconstitutional, in violation of the First Amendment in that it brought religious indoctrination into the schools. The theological battle has continued to have its ups and downs ever since the days of Lyman Abbott and Charles Hodge. Some of the basic questions raised may, of course, never be fully resolved to the satisfaction of all.

The Bible and Evolution

The Scopes trial was almost as much a trial of the Bible as it was of a single teacher. Were those who favored evolution automatically enemies of the Bible? Was Bryan the best defender the Bible could have? These questions were dealt with directly in that same decade of the 1920s. The *New York Times* asked Bryan to offer his views on this matter. Then the Reverend Harry Emerson Fosdick (1878–1969), pastor of a leading New York church at the time, was asked to reply. The selections given here inquire specifically into the use of the Bible as a book of science. As you read the selections by Bryan and Fosdick, keep in mind the following:

1. For Bryan the Bible's authority is to be applied to what areas of life or of learning?
2. For Fosdick, in what areas of the Bible is teaching most needed?
3. How, says Fosdick, does Bryan degrade the Bible?
4. Which argument seems better set forth? Why? Note strengths or weaknesses in each.

William Jennings Bryan[9]

I object to Darwinism [theory of evolution] because it has not one syllable in the Bible to support it. This ought to make Christians cautious

8 By permission of *Liveright*, Publishers, New York. Copyright ©1955 by Mrs. Jane Butler.

9 Adapted from the *New York Times*, February 26, 1922.

William Jennings Bryan, one of the opponents of the theory of evolution, and his wife Mary in 1906.

about accepting it without thorough investigation. The Bible not only describes man's creation but gives a reason for it. Man is a part of God's plan and is placed on earth for a purpose. Both the Old and the New Testament deal with man and with man only. Is it not strange that a Christian will accept Darwinism as a substitute for the Bible when the Bible not only does not support Darwin's hypothesis but directly and expressly contradicts it? . . .

Darwinism entirely changes one's view of life and undermines faith in the Bible. Evolution has no place for the miracle or the supernatural. Evolution attempts to solve the mystery of life by suggesting a process of development commencing "in the dawn of time" and continuing uninterrupted up until now. Evolution does not explain creation. It simply diverts attention from it by hiding it behind eons of time. If a man accepts Darwinism and is consistent, he rejects the miracle and the supernatural as impossible. He begins with the first chapter of Genesis and blots out the story of man's creation—not because the evidence is insufficient—but because the miracle is inconsistent with evolution. . . .

Let those believers in "the tree man" come down out of the trees and meet the issue. Let them defend the teachings of agnosticism[10] or theism[11] if they dare. If they deny that the natural tendency of Darwinism is to lead many to a denial of God, let them frankly point out the portions of the Bible which they regard as consistent with Darwinism. These believers weaken faith in God, discourage prayer, raise doubt as to future life, reduce Christ to the stature of a man, and make the Bible a "scrap of paper."

Harry Emerson Fosdick[12]

My reply to Mr. Bryan is concerned with the theological rather than the scientific aspects of his statement. There seems to be no doubt about what his position is. He proposes to take his science from the Bible. Mr. Bryan says, "Is it not strange that Christians will accept Darwinism as a substitute for the Bible when the Bible not only does not support Darwin's hypothesis, but directly and expressly contradicts it?" What other interpretation of such a statement is possible except this? Namely, that the Bible is for Mr. Bryan an authoritative textbook in biology. And if the Bible is authoritative in biology, then why not in astronomy, geology, chemistry or any other science whatever?

Martin Luther attacked Copernicus[13] with the same appeal which Mr. Bryan uses. Luther said, "This fool wishes to reverse the entire science of astronomy, but sacred Scripture tells us that Joshua commanded the sun to stand still, and not the earth." Nor was Martin Luther wrong if the Bible is indeed an authoritative textbook in science. A denial that the earth moves around the sun can unquestionably be found in the Bible if one starts out to use the Bible in that way. . . .

As a teacher and preacher of religion, however, I must protest against all this. I protest because this kind of reasoning does such gross injustice to the Bible. There is no book to compare with the Bible. The world never needed more its fundamental principles of life, its fully developed views of God and man, its finest faiths and hopes and loves.

When one reads an article like Mr. Bryan's, one feels not that the Bible is being defended, but that it is being attacked. Is a cello being

---

10 *Agnosticism*—the belief that one cannot know the existence of God with certainty.

11 *Theism*—the belief that God is better known through nature and the natural order than through miracles or special revelations.

12 Adapted from the *New York Times*, March 12, 1922.

13 Nicolaus Copernicus (1473-1543). Polish astronomer who upset traditional thinking and caused much controversy with his finding that the sun, not the earth, is the center of our solar system.

defended when instead of being used for music it is advertised as a good dinner table? Mr. Bryan does a similar disservice to the Bible. Instead of using it for what it is—the most noble, useful, inspiring and inspired book of spiritual life which we have—he sets it up for what it is not and was never meant to be. He treats the Bible as a fixed measure by which all human thought is to be cut and trimmed.

Mr. Bryan and others of his school hate evolution because they fear it will lower the dignity of man. Just what do they mean? Even in the Book of Genesis God made man out of the dust of the earth. Surely, that is low enough to start and evolution starts no lower. So long as God is the creative power, what difference does it make whether out of the dust by sudden command or out of the dust by gradual process God brought man into being? Here man is, and what he is he is. Were it decided that God had dropped him from the sky, he would still be the man he is. If it is decided that God brought him up by slow gradations out of lower forms of life, he still is the man he is.

The fact is that the process by which man came to be upon the planet is a very important scientific problem, but it is not a crucially important religious problem. Origins prove nothing in the realm of values. To all persons of spiritual insight, man—no matter by what process he at first arrived—is the child of God, made in His image, destined for His character.

Creationism and the Classroom

The latest tangle between religion and science arises from the efforts of some to teach biblical creationism *as science*. It is appropriate to teach biblical creationism along with other widely held religious views in other areas of the curriculum, such as the humanities or social studies. Academic instruction *about* religion as distinct from indoctrination *in* religion is a legitimate responsibility of all education, public or private. It is important for students to know about religious institutions, ideas, and influences. The courts do not object to any activities of this kind.

The courts do get involved, however, when a particular sectarian or denominational position is set forth in government supported (public) schools. Private schools, of course, whether church-related or not, have much wider freedom in this regard, and the courts, once again, tend not to get involved as long as certain standards of health, safety, and educational quality are maintained. Our concern in this section, therefore, is a narrow and limited one: the teaching in the public school of religious views that are judged to be private or sectarian in nature. Creationism, which is sometimes also called creation science, has been found to fall into the latter category.

In 1981, the U.S. District Judge in the state of Arkansas concluded that a law passed earlier that year was unconstitutional because it advanced the views associated with a particular religious position. The law (Act 590) promoted ideas "inspired by the Book of Genesis," and so the judge declared that "without a doubt a major effect of the Act is the advancement of particular religious beliefs." That would make the law unconstitutional, since federal courts had taken the position in several other decisions that for a law to be constitutional its primary effect must be secular rather than religious.

In 1987 a similar law that had been passed in the State of Louisiana was decided by the U.S. Supreme Court (*Edwards* v. *Aguillard*). As you read a portion from the majority opinion, consider the following questions:

1. The full title of Louisiana's Creationism Act is "Balanced Treatment for Creation-Science and Evolution-Science in Public School Instruction." What does the Supreme Court say about the concept of balance or fairness?
2. Why did the Supreme Court (in a 7 to 2 vote) find this Louisiana Act to be unconstitutional?

If the Louisiana legislature's purpose was solely to maximize the comprehensiveness and effectiveness of science instruction, it would have encouraged the teaching of all scientific theories about the origins of humankind. But under the Act's requirements, teachers who were once free to teach any and all facets of this subject are now unable to do so. Moreover, the Act fails even to ensure that any creation science will be taught, but instead requires the teaching of this theory only when the theory of evolution is taught. Thus we agree . . . that the Act does not serve to protect academic freedom, but has the distinctly different purpose of discrediting "evolution by counterbalancing its teaching at every turn with the teaching of creation science." . . .

Furthermore, it is not happenstance that the legislature required the teaching of a theory that coincided with this religious view. The legislative history documents that the Act's primary purpose was to change the science curriculum of public schools in order to provide persuasive advantage to a particular religious doctrine that rejects the factual basis of evolution in its entirety. The sponsor of the Creationism Act, Senator [Bill] Keith, explained during the legislative hearings that his disdain for the theory of evolution resulted from the support that

Religious instruction is provided in a program of dismissed time just off the school grounds in Fort Wayne, Indiana, 1964.

evolution supplied to views contrary to his own religious beliefs. . . . Because the primary purpose of the Creationism Act is to advance a particular religious belief, the Act endorses religion in violation of the First Amendment.[14]

Justice White and Justice O'Connor agreed with the majority opinion but wrote a separate opinion in which they emphasized that there should be sensitivity to the religious heritage of the country and that various references to that heritage "are constitutionally acceptable." They added that "as a matter of history, school children can and should be properly informed of all aspects of the nation's religious heritage." They went on to say that students should be taught about the religious beliefs of the Founding Fathers "and how these beliefs affected the attitudes of the times and the structures of our government." They concluded that "since religion permeates our history, a familiarity with the nature of religious beliefs is necessary to understand many historical as well as contemporary events."[15]

Justice Scalia and Justice Rehnquist dissented from the view of the majority, arguing that the case was wrongly decided. As you read the summary paragraph below, consider the following questions:

14 *Journal of Church and State* (Autumn, 1987), pp. 611, 612, 613.

15 *Journal of Church and State* (Autumn, 1987), pp. 619-620.

1. How does one determine the question of "primary purpose" in evaluating the action of a state (or federal) legislature?
2. What do the dissenters mean by "Scopes-in-reverse"? Discuss.

In sum, even if one concedes for the sake of argument that a majority of the Louisiana Legislature voted for the Balanced Treatment Act partly in order to foster (rather than merely eliminate discrimination against) Christian fundamentalist beliefs, our cases establish that that alone would not suffice to invalidate the Act, so long as there was a genuine secular purpose as well. We have, moreover, no adequate basis for disbelieving the secular purpose set forth in the Act itself, or for concluding that it is a sham enacted to conceal the legislators' violation of their oaths of office. I am astonished by the Court's unprecedented readiness to reach such a conclusion, which I can only attribute to an intellectual predisposition created by the facts and the legend of [the Scopes trial]—an instinctive reaction that any governmentally imposed requirements bearing upon the teaching of evolution must be a manifestation of Christian fundamentalist repression. In this case, however, it seems to me the Court's position is the repressive one. The people of Louisiana, including those who are Christian fundamentalists, are quite entitled, as a secular matter, to have whatever scientific evidence there may be against evolution presented in their schools, just as Mr. Scopes was entitled to present whatever scientific evidence there was for it. Perhaps what the Louisiana Legislature has done is unconstitutional because there *is* no such evidence, and the scheme they have established will amount to no more than a presentation of the Book of Genesis. But we cannot say that on the evidence before us in this summary judgment context, which includes ample uncontradicted testimony that "creation science" is a body of scientific knowledge rather than revealed belief. *Infinitely less* can we say (or should we say) that the scientific evidence for evolution is so conclusive that no one could be gullible enough to believe that there is any real scientific evidence to the contrary, so that the legislation's purpose must be a lie. Yet that illiberal judgment, that Scopes-in-reverse, is ultimately the basis on which the Court's facile rejection of the Louisiana Legislature's purpose must rest.[16]

Final Note: This study makes no attempt to present or evaluate the *scientific* aspects of evolution. This is not the task of social studies. Rather, the study seeks to show the *impact* of evolutionary theory on American culture, thought, and religion in the nineteenth and twentieth centuries.

16 *Journal of Church and State* (Autumn, 1987), p. 631.

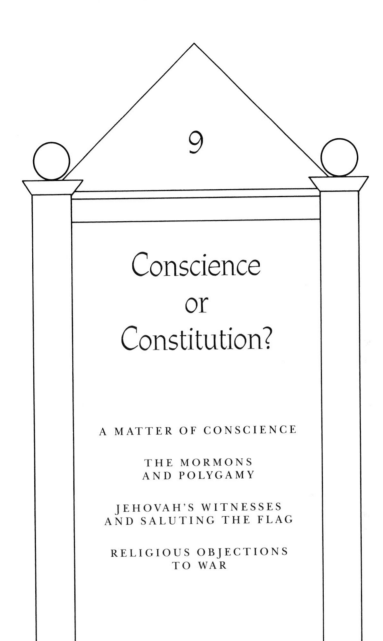

9

Conscience
or
Constitution?

A MATTER OF CONSCIENCE

THE MORMONS
AND POLYGAMY

JEHOVAH'S WITNESSES
AND SALUTING THE FLAG

RELIGIOUS OBJECTIONS
TO WAR

A Matter of Conscience

Being Conscious of Conscience

Some of the boys planned to take their dates out to the strip—a stretch of nightclubs, bars, and dance halls along the oceanfront—after the Junior-Senior Prom. Bill had never taken a girl out there before and was somewhat reluctant to join the plan.

"Come on," said his best friend Jack. "You've got nothing to lose. Besides, Linda will think you're more of a man than if you take her to that dumb party at the Teen Center."

"And," interrupted his pal Steve, "you'll miss seeing that new hard rock band if you don't go."

"I can't," replied Bill. "Linda's folks would have fits if they thought we were going there."

"Look, they'll never know. Who's going to tell them what's happening after the prom?" asked Jack.

"Yeah, nobody will find out," added Steve.

"I know that," said Bill, "but Linda's parents trust me. *My conscience would bother me.*"

"Hey Susie, why the blank look on your face?" asked Carol.

"Oh, I'm trying to figure out what to do about Friday night," she answered.

"What's to figure out?"

"Well," sighed Susie, "Randy finally asked me to go to the game over at Johnson City—and I said yes, of course."

"Wow, and you'd get to ride over in his new MG!"

"Yeah, but I'd already told Alvin Brown I would go with him—on the bus."

"You mean you made dates with both of them for the same game?"

"That's the problem. I really want to go with Randy. But I did make the date with Alvin first. What am I going to do?"

"All I can say is *let your conscience be your guide.*"

"Mr Anderson is easy to fool. Too bad you don't have him for English," said Joe.

"What do you mean?" asked Arthur.

"He believes just about anything you tell him. Yesterday I said I had to go to the office to see about a lost gym suit. He never even checked to see if I went there. I spent almost the whole period smoking out in the parking lot with Eddy. And last week I told him I had to call home because my mother was sick. I never did go back to his class that day."

"What did he say?"

"Next day he asked how my mother was feeling. Really. Boy, is he dumb!"

"You know—*you have no conscience at all.*"

"Hey, Sam, what's the matter with your father?" asked Paul. "When I called this morning he sounded real bugged. He started griping about today's kids having no appreciation for what they got, no guts, and stuff like that."

"Oh, that. He's all weirded out about my oldest brother, Ralph, refusing to register for the draft. He says we're disgraced because we have a traitor and coward in the family," explained Sam.

"Why's your brother acting that way? I think anybody who refuses to register should be called a traitor and coward," declared Paul.

"No, he shouldn't. He's a conscientious objector."

"What's that?" asked Paul.

"It means," replied Sam, "that he won't fight because he doesn't believe in war. It goes *against his conscience.*"

"That doesn't make his actions right," Sam shot back. "My conscience tells me that a man is duty-bound to fight for his country. As far as I'm concerned, your brother *doesn't even have a conscience!*"

"Hey, stop the car!" shouted Louis.

"Why? What for" asked Jim.

"I think there's a cat limping on the side of the road. I bet he's been hit by a car. See, over there," Louis answered as he pointed out the window.

"We haven't got time to stop for an old cat," groaned Jim impatiently. "We're late as it is. The girls will be mad if we miss the beginning of the show. Besides, it looked all right to me."

"No, stop. I've got to find out if it's hurt or not. Back up to where it was," directed Louis.

"OK, OK," sighed Jim. "Do you see it yet?"

"Yeah, and it seems all right."

"Are you satisfied? Can we go now?" asked Jim.

"I just wanted to make sure it wasn't badly hurt. If we didn't stop it would have bothered me."

"You sure are soft-hearted—a real sissy," said Jim.

"No, not a sissy," Louis calmly replied, "but I do have a *guilty conscience* when I don't do something that I think I should. Maybe that's just as bad as being a sissy."

The above situations illustrate the function of that uniquely human quality called conscience. Of course, consideration of conscience is not limited to the trials and tribulations of daily living. Matters of conscience have raised people to positions of glory and prominence. They have also condemned them to scorn and oblivion. Obedience to the dictates of conscience has resulted in the martyrdom of men such as Socrates and women such as Joan of Arc. The obligations of conscience have stimulated the most noble of acts and, as we may judge them, the most infamous of deeds.

The Quality Called Conscience

FIVE VIEWS OF CONSCIENCE

Conscience has won the highest praise of poets and philosophers, but it has also been derided by them. Some have claimed infallibility for conscience. Others have pointed out its inadequacy. Below are five quotations. You will notice that the attitudes toward conscience are quite different. After you have read them be prepared to discuss the following:

1. What is said in each quotation? (Put the thoughts into your own words.)
2. Do you agree or disagree with each quotation? Why?

"Conscience was born when man had shed his fur, his tail, his pointed ears."
—SIR RICHARD BURTON, *The Kasidah*, Pt. V, St. 19.

"The laws of conscience, which we pretend are born of nature, are born of custom." —MONTAIGNE, *Essays*, Bk. I, Ch. 22.

"Conscience is but a word that cowards use, devised at first to keep the strong in awe." —SHAKESPEARE, *King Richard III*, Act V, Sc. 3, Line 310.

"A man's conscience and his judgment is the same thing, and as the judgment, so also the conscience may be erroneous."
—THOMAS HOBBES, *Leviathan*, Pt. II, Ch. 29.

"God has given to every man an unalienable right in matters of His worship to act for himself as his conscience receives its direction from God."
—PETITIONERS TO THE GENERAL COURT OF MASSACHUSETTS,
June 7, 1749.

THE NATURE OF CONSCIENCE

The above quotations indicate that no agreement exists as to the nature of conscience. It has demanded the attention of theologians, philosophers, psychologists, and many others who have asked questions such as the following:

Is conscience emotional or rational?
Is it conscious or unconscious?
Is it universal and unchanging or is it determined by time and place?
Is conscience always a right guide or can it be wrong?

Of particular concern has been the source of conscience, for in the source of conscience one finds the authority of conscience. Holy writings, the "Word of God," eternal verities, "natural law," custom and traditions, common sense, and rationality—all of these have been cited as the authority upon which conscience depends, and for many people, each may constitute that authority.

THE USE OF CONSCIENCE

Conscience, it must be remembered, is not mere awareness of right and wrong. Together with awareness, conscience includes a feeling of obligation to be or to do that which is recognized as right or good. This feeling of obligation becomes so strong that failure to meet it may result in a so-called guilty conscience. People may even feel inwardly compelled to confess such guilt to others in order to soothe the conscience. In extreme cases, a troubled conscience may cause physical or mental illness in individuals. Of course, conscience is not necessarily a negative influence. People do take positive action guided by their consciences. Successful meeting of the conscience-obligation usually results in feelings of satisfaction and well-being. Individuals who follow their conscience even when it means loss of wealth, prestige, or recognition often gain a measure of self-respect and fulfillment far more valuable than the fleeting pleasures of the moment.

A CONFLICT OF CONSCIENCE

Human behavior based on conscience is considered by most Americans to be worthy of the highest praise. Those people unable or unwilling to follow conscience in doing what they know to be right are generally condemned. How do we react, however, when we observe people following their conscience in behavior that is unacceptable to us? In other words, what happens when two groups of people living together in a society arrive at opposite conclusions regarding what is meant by good or bad behavior? Could we, as a third party, step in and simply say, "Let your conscience be your guide" even if we know that hostilities will result if each follows our advice or even if we know that this could threaten the existence of the society? There are no easy answers to such questions. The basic principles of our way of life are put to the severest test when action based on conscience places people in conflict with others or the laws of the land. On the one hand Americans are committed to the preservation of a stable society necessary for the general welfare of its members; on the other hand, Americans are committed under the Bill of Rights to defend the free exercise of religion—a right that many regard as a freedom to obey conscience.

These questions of conscience are so important and so vexing to Americans that they have been sent all the way to the U.S. Supreme Court for solution. By examining the words of those who have had to wrestle with such problems, we can gain an appreciation of the complexity of the legal and moral issues. The readings that follow help us understand the careful judgments and wise methods that are necessary to resolve questions of conscience.

The Mormons and Polygamy

In 1830, Joseph Smith started a new religious group that came to be officially called the Church of Jesus Christ of Latter-day Saints. The Mormons,[1] as members of this church were unofficially and popularly known, moved from New York to Ohio to Missouri to Illinois where Joseph Smith was assassinated in 1844. After this, Brigham Young assumed leadership in the new church, leading most of the members out of Illinois into the great plains and deserts of the West. The Mormons settled in Utah territory and soon made the desert bloom. Salt Lake City became, and remains, the national center of the Church of Jesus Christ of Latter-day Saints.

The Mormons moved a good deal in their earlier years. The principal reason for this was the hostility and suspicion that often met Mormons wherever they went. What accounts for the hostility? Mormons lived in a group to themselves, following practices and holding beliefs different from their neighbors. Being different is by itself often enough to arouse

1 So called from the sacred book, *Book of Mormon,* published by Joseph Smith in 1830.

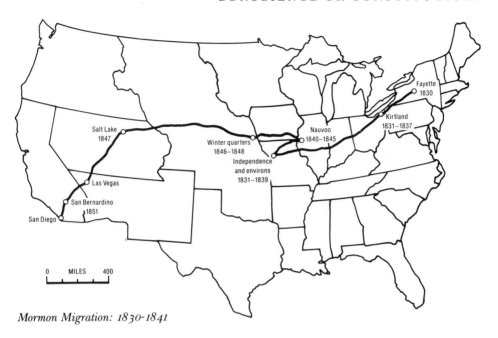

Mormon Migration: 1830-1841

suspicion. But the nature of the difference is important, too. Within the Mormon community, no one owned private property; all real estate and businesses were held in common. Some neighbors regarded this as peculiar or strange. Theologically, this new church offered doctrinal interpretations that radically challenged traditional Christianity. More immediately disturbing, however, was the fact that several men in this new church had more than one wife. This practice of polygamy created storms of protest and resistance.

So the Mormons moved. When they reached the territory of Utah, they thought that they were far enough away from all neighbors to be able to live as they wished. But the population in the East kept migrating west. As more people moved west, more and more territories became states, accepting the Constitution and laws of the United States. Even as territories, however, these western lands came under the jurisdiction of Congress. In 1862, Congress passed a law making bigamy[2] or polygamy a crime in the territories. Thus the whole question of plural marriages, as the Mormon practice was often called, became something more than a matter of custom or opinion. It became a matter for the courts and the country.

In 1879, the U.S. Supreme Court handed down its opinion on a case of bigamy. The second marriage was clearly based on religious doctrine.

---

2 *Bigamy*—a second marriage while the first marriage is still in effect, literally "two wives."

Indeed, it was performed by an official of the Church of Jesus Christ of Latter-day Saints. The second marriage, the defense argued, had been entered into as a religious duty, without criminal intent, and therefore the defendent should be found not guilty. To see what the Supreme Court decided, read the following selection.

As you read Chief Justice Waite's opinion in the Reynolds case (1879), keep in mind the following:

1. What did the Supreme court decide?
2. What "chain of reasoning" does Justice Waite use in arriving at this conclusion?
3. What information does Justice Waite supply to support the claim that the law in question is valid?
4. What examples of behavior does Justice Waite use to illustrate his contention that denial of practice of religion is valid? Why might he choose these particular examples?
5. What does Justice Waite imply would happen to society if the Mormons were allowed to follow their conscience? Does this prediction seem valid?

Reynolds v. United States (1879)

Mr. Chief Justice Waite delivered the opinion of the Court.

. . . Should the accused have been acquitted if he married the second time, because he believed it to be his religious duty?

. . . the question is raised whether religious belief can be accepted as a justification of an overt act made criminal by the law of the land. The inquiry is not as to the power of Congress to prescribe criminal laws for the Territories, but as to the guilt of one who knowingly violates a law which has been properly enacted, if he entertains a belief that the law is wrong.

Congress cannot pass a law for the government of the Territories which shall prohibit the free exercise of religion. The first amendment to the Constitution expressly forbids such legislation. Religious freedom is guaranteed everywhere throughout the United States, so far as congressional interference is concerned. The question to be determined is whether the law now under consideration comes within the prohibition.

. . . Polygamy has always been odious [offensive] among the Northern and Western nations of Europe and, until the establishment of the Mormon Church, was almost exclusively a feature of the life of Asiatic

Mormons in Utah hauling wood down from the mountains, around 1870.

and African people. At common law, the second marriage was always void, and from the earliest history of England polygamy has been treated as an offense against society. . . . there never was a time in any State of the Union when polygamy has not been an offense against society. . . . In the face of all this evidence, it is impossible to believe that the constitutional guaranty of religious freedom was intended to prohibit legislation in respect to this most important feature of social life. Marriage, while from its very nature a sacred obligation, is nevertheless in most civilized nations a civil contract, and usually regulated by law. Upon it society may be said to be built. . . .

In our opinion the statute [against bigamy] is within the legislative power of Congress. It is constitutional and valid. . . . This being so, the only question which remains is whether those who make polygamy a part of their religion are excepted from the operation of the statute. . . . Laws are made for the government of actions, and while they cannot interfere with mere religious belief and opinions, they may with practices. Suppose one believed that human sacrifices were a necessary part of religious worship. Would it be seriously contended that the civil government under which he lived could not interfere to prevent a sacrifice? Or if a wife religiously believed it was her duty to burn herself upon the funeral pyre of her dead husband, would it be beyond the power of the civil government to prevent her carrying her belief into practice?

So here . . . it is provided that plural marriages shall not be allowed. Can a man excuse his practices to the contrary because of his religious belief? To permit this would be to make the professed doctrines of religious belief superior to the law of the land, and in effect to permit every citizen to become a law unto himself. Government could exist only in name under such circumstances.

Jehovah's Witnesses and Saluting The Flag

In Allegheny, Pennsylvania, Charles Taze Russell in 1872 organized a small group of followers into what later came to be called Jehovah's Witnesses. Emphasizing that the world would soon be coming to an end, the Witnesses grew rapidly from a tiny band in Pennsylvania to about a million members less than a century later. That membership, moreover, was worldwide, with pioneers and publishers, as their missionary workers are called, active in both hemispheres.

The Witnesses have attracted much attention through their vigorous missionary efforts. Door-to-door salesmanship is out of fashion for most religious groups in America today, but not for the Witnesses. The group also has a publication program of enormous scope. Millions of copies of pamphlets, periodicals, and books are sold on street corners, studied in the meetings of the congregations, or given away to those unwilling or unable to buy them.

Greatest attention has come to the Witnesses, however, through their frequent brushes with the law. A number of charges have been brought against them: refusal to serve in the armed forces, disturbing the peace, selling without a license, preaching in public parks, and so on. Time after time, cases involving the Witnesses have reached all the way to the Supreme Court. So many arrests were made—over a thousand per year by 1940— that the official headquarters in Brooklyn, New York, found it necessary to develop its own legal division.

The case that attracted the most attention and raised the most crucial questions involved the refusal to salute the American flag.

Two young children, William (age ten) and Lillian (age twelve) Gobitis, attended the public schools of Pennsylvania where the pledge of allegiance to the flag was offered each morning. Upon instructions from their parents, who were Jehovah's Witnesses, William and Lillian did not join in the daily ceremony. The public school required the performance of the ceremony on patriotic grounds. The Gobitis children refused to comply

During services in Harlan County Kentucky in 1942, followers test their faith by handling snakes. The government often intervened to end this practice, which challenges the bounds of religious freedom.

on religious grounds. They believed that the flag salute was an act of idolatry specifically forbidden by scripture. The school district then declined to accept them as pupils, forcing the parents to place their children in a private school. The parents brought suit against the school district, and eventually the case—*Minersville School District* v. *Gobitis*—reached the United States Supreme Court in 1940.

The matter did not end there, however. In 1943, another case—*West Virginia State Board of Education* v. *Barnette*—was brought before the Supreme Court, and it went through the same general arguments but reversed its 1940 position. Furthermore, in both cases the Supreme Court was itself divided. Strong dissenting opinions—that is, opinions that differed from the majority of the nine justices—were voiced in each instance. Thus, it was a more complex case than that which dealt with polygamy. To show that complexity more clearly, both the majority and dissenting judicial views for the two cases are presented below.

As you read the four opinions of the two cases involving the Jehovah's Witnesses, keep in mind the following:

1. In the Gobitis case, what does Justice Frankfurter feel to be the most important concern?

2. How does Justice Stone disagree with the majority opinion? What arguments does he use?
3. In the Barnette case, what is the greatest danger foreseen by Justice Jackson if activities such as the flag salute are made compulsory?
4. How has Justice Frankfurter's emphasis changed in writing his Barnette decision as compared to Gobitis?

Minersville School District v. *Gobitis (1940)*

Majority Opinion

The majority opinion was delivered by Mr. Justice Frankfurter.

A grave responsibility confronts this Court whenever in course of litigation [carrying on a lawsuit] it must reconcile the conflicting claims of liberty and authority. But when the liberty invoked is liberty of conscience, and the authority is authority to safeguard the nation's fellowship, judicial conscience is put to its severest test. Of such nature is the present controversy.

Lillian Gobitis, aged twelve, and her brother William, aged ten, were expelled from the public schools of Minersville, Pennsylvania, for refusing to salute the national flag as part of a daily school exercise. The local Board of Education required both teachers and pupils to participate in this ceremony. The ceremony is a familiar one. The right hand is placed on the breast and the following pledge recited in unison: "I pledge allegiance to my flag, and to the Republic for which it stands; one nation indivisible, with liberty and justice for all."[3] . . . The Gobitis family are affiliated with "Jehovah's Witnesses," for whom the Bible as the Word of God is the supreme authority. The children had been brought up conscientiously to believe that such a gesture of respect for the flag was forbidden by command of Scripture. . . .

Situations like the present are phases of the profoundest problem confronting a democracy—the problem which Lincoln cast in memorable dilemma. "Must a government of necessity be too strong for the liberties of its people, or too weak to maintain its own existence?" . . .

The ultimate foundation of a free society is the binding tie of cohesive sentiment. Such a sentiment is fostered by all those agencies of the mind and spirit which may serve to gather up the traditions of a people, transmit them from generation to generation, and thereby create that continuity of a treasured common life which constitutes a

3 An earlier form of the familiar pledge.

civilization. "We live by symbols." The flag is the symbol of our national unity, transcending all internal differences, however large, within the framework of the Constitution. This Court has had occasion to say that ". . . the flag is the symbol of the Nation's power, the emblem of freedom in its truest, best sense . . ."

. . . The precise issue, then, for us to decide is whether the legislatures of the various states and the authorities in a thousand counties and school districts of this country are barred from calling forth that unifying sentiment. Without such a sentiment there can ultimately be no liberties, civil or religious. . . .

The preciousness of the family relation, the authority and independence which give dignity to parenthood, indeed the enjoyment of all freedom, depends upon the kind of ordered society which is summarized by our flag. A society which is dedicated to the preservation of these ultimate values of civilization may protect itself. It may use the educational process to bring about those almost unconscious feelings which bind men together. That is to say, the educational process may be used so long as men's right to believe as they please, to win others to their way of belief, and their right to assemble in their chosen places of worship for the devotional[4] ceremonies of their faith, are fully respected. . . . [The "process" in this case was saluting the flag. The Justice concluded that it was constitutional for a school district to require the salute.]

Dissenting Opinion

The dissenting opinion was delivered by Mr. Justice Stone.

. . . the constitutional guaranties of personal liberty are not always absolutes. Government has a right to survive and powers conferred upon it are not necessarily cancelled out by prohibitions of the Bill of Rights. It may make war and raise armies. To that end it may compel citizens to give military service, and subject them to military training despite their religious objections.

Government may suppress religious practices dangerous to morals, and presumably those also which are dangerous to public safety, health and good order. But it is a long step, and one which I am unable to take, to the position that government may, as a supposed educational measure, compel public declarations which violate children's religious conscience.

4 *Devotional*—worshipful; prayerful; having to do with acts of piety or devotion.

. . . there are other ways to teach loyalty and patriotism, which are the sources of national unity. These other ways must not force the pupil to affirm [declare positively] that which he does not believe or command him to offer a declaration which violates his religious convictions. Without turning to such compulsion, the state is free to compel attendance at school. It is also free to require the teaching and study of those things in our history and in the structure and organization of our government which tend to inspire patriotism and love of country. . . .

The guaranties of civil liberty are but guaranties of freedom of the human mind and spirit and of reasonable freedom and opportunity to express them. They assume the right of the individual to hold such opinions as he will and to give them reasonably free expression. They also assume the individual's freedom, and that of the state as well, to teach and persuade others by the communication of ideas. The very essence of the liberty which they guaranty is the freedom of the individual from compulsion as to what he shall think and what he shall say, at least where the compulsion is to bear false witness to his religion. If these guaranties are to have any meaning they must, I think, withhold from the state any authority to compel belief or the expression of it where that expression violates religious convictions.

History teaches us that there have been but few invasions of personal liberty by the state which have not been justified, as they are here, in the name of righteousness and the public good. Also, most such invasions have been directed, as they are now, at politically helpless minorities. The framers of the Constitution prescribed as limitations upon the powers of government the freedom of the mind and spirit secured by the explicit guaranties of freedom of speech and religion. In so doing, they left no room for a legislative judgment that the compulsory expression of belief which violates religious convictions would better serve the public interest than their protection. . . . [The Justice therefore believed that religious convictions should be protected, even if the American flag went unsaluted.]

West Virginia State Board of Education v. Barnette (1943)

Majority Opinion

The majority opinion was delivered by Mr. Justice Jackson.

. . . The Witnesses are an unincorporated body teaching that the obligation imposed by the law of God is superior to that of laws enacted by temporal government. Their religious beliefs include a literal version of *Exodus*, Chapter 20, verses 4 and 5, which says: "Thou shalt not make unto thee any graven image, or any likeness of anything that is in heaven above, or that is in the earth beneath, or that is in the water under the earth; thou shalt not bow down thyself to them nor serve them." They consider that the flag is an "image" within this command. For this reason they refuse to salute it.

Children of this faith have been expelled from school and are threatened with exclusion for no other cause. Officials threaten to send them to reformatories maintained for criminally inclined juveniles. Parents of such children have been prosecuted and are threatened with prosecutions for causing delinquency. . . .

Lastly, the Gobitis opinion [of 1940] reasons that "National unity is the basis of national security." That opinion also argued that state and school authorities have the right to decide how that unity is to be reached. Then, the court concluded that compulsory measures which promote "national unity" are constitutional. This is the heart of our argument with that earlier opinion.

We do not question that national unity may be promoted by persuasion and example. We do question whether compulsion, as in the saluting of the flag, is a permissible means under the Constitution for achieving that unity.

Struggles to require uniformity of sentiment in support of some end have been waged by many good as well as by evil men. Nationalism is a relatively recent phenomenon, but at other times and places the ends have been racial or territorial security, support of a dynasty or regime, and particular plans for saving souls. As first and moderate methods to attain unity have failed, those determined to accomplish unity must resort to an ever increasing harshness. As governmental pressure toward unity becomes greater, so strife becomes more bitter as to whose "united" position will win. Probably no deeper division of our people could result from any cause than from public educational officials compelling youth to unite in embracing some doctrine or program. . . . Those who begin a forceful elimination of dissent[5] soon find themselves exterminating dissenters. Compulsory unification of opinion achieves only the unanimity[6] of the graveyard.

It seems trite but necessary to say that the First Amendment to our Constitution was designed to avoid these ends by avoiding these beginnings. There is no mystery in the American concept of the State

5 *Dissent*—disagreement with prevailing opinion.

6 *Unanimity*—the state of being unanimous, or in agreement

or of the nature or origin of its authority. We set up government by consent of the governed, and the Bill of Rights denies those in power any legal opportunity to coerce that consent. Authority here is to be controlled by public opinion, not public opinion by authority.

The case is made difficult not because the principles of its decision are obscure but because the flag involved is our own. Nevertheless, we apply the limitations of the Constitution with no fear that freedom to be intellectually and spiritually diverse [different] or even contrary [opposed] will disintegrate the social organization. To believe that patriotism will not flourish if patriotic ceremonies are voluntary and spontaneous instead of a compulsory routine is to make an unflattering estimate of the appeal of our institutions to free minds. . . . But freedom to differ is not limited to things that do not matter much. That would be a mere shadow of freedom. The test of its substance is the right to differ as to things that touch the heart of the existing order.

If there is any fixed star in our constitutional constellation, it is that no official, high or petty, can prescribe what shall be orthodox in politics, nationalism, religion, or other matters of opinion or force citizens to confess by word or act their faith therein. If there are any circumstances which permit an exception, they do not now occur to us.

We think the action of the local authorities in compelling the flag and pledge goes beyond constitutional limitations on their power and invades the sphere of intellect and spirit which it is the purpose of the First Amendment to our Constitution to reserve from all official control. [Reversing the 1940 decision, the Court here decides that public school children shall not be compelled to salute the flag, if such a salute would be a violation of their religious convictions.]

Dissenting Opinion

The dissenting opinion was delivered by Mr. Justice Frankfurter.

One who belongs to the most abused and persecuted minority [the Jews] in history is not likely to be insensible to the freedoms guaranteed by our Constitution. Were my purely personal attitude relevant I should whole-heartedly associate myself with the general libertarian[7] views in the Court's opinion, representing as they do the thought and action of a lifetime. But as judges we are neither Jew nor Gentile, neither Catholic or agnostic.[8] We owe equal attachment to the Constitution and

7 *Libertarian*—favoring individual rights and liberties.

8 *Agnosticism*—the belief that one cannot know the existence of God with certainty.

are equally bound by our judicial obligations whether we derive our citizenship from the earliest or the latest immigrants to these shores. As a member of this Court I am not justified in writing my private notions of policy into the Constitution, no matter how deeply I may cherish them or how mischievous I may view their disregard. The duty of a judge who must decide which of two claims before the Court shall prevail . . . is not that of the ordinary person. It can never be emphasized too much that one's own opinion about the wisdom or evil of a law should be excluded altogether when one is doing one's duty on the bench. . . .

The constitutional protection of religious freedom ended disabilities, it did not create new privileges. It gave religious equality, not civil immunity [exemption]. Its essence is freedom from conformity to religious dogma, not freedom from conformity to law because of religious dogma. . . .

The prohibition against any religious establishment by the government placed denominations on an equal footing—it assured freedom from support by the government to any mode of worship and the freedom of individuals to support any mode of worship. Any person may therefore believe or disbelieve what he pleases. He may practice what he will in his own house of worship or publicly within the limits of public order. But the lawmaking authority is not limited by the variety of religious beliefs. Otherwise the constitutional guaranty would be not a protection of the free exercise of religion but a denial of the exercise of legislation.

The essence of the religious freedom guaranteed by our Constitution is therefore this: no religion shall either receive the state's support or meet with its hostility. Religion is outside the sphere of political government. This does not mean that all matters on which religious organizations or beliefs may pronounce are outside the sphere of government. Were this so, instead of the separation of church and state, there would be the subordination of the state on any matter assumed to be within the sovereignty of the religious conscience. . . .

Saluting the flag suppresses no belief nor curbs it. Children and their parents may believe what they please, proclaim their belief and practice it. Saluting the flag involves no restriction against the fullest opportunity on the part both of the children and of their parents to disclaim publicly (as they choose to do so) the meaning that others attach to the gesture of salute. All channels of affirmative free expression are open to both children and parents. Had we before us any act of the state putting the slightest curbs upon such free expression, I should not lag behind any member of this Court in striking down such

The struggle for women's rights was a matter of conscience as well as principle. Here in 1913, a suffragette parade in Washington, D.C. makes its point. (The Nineteenth Amendment, which granted the vote to women, was ratified in 1920.)

an invasion of the right to freedom of thought and freedom of speech protected by the Constitution.

I am strengthened in my view of this case by the history of the flag salute controversy in this Court. Five times has the precise question now before us been judged. Four times the Court unanimously found that the requirement of such a school exercise was not beyond the powers of the states. . . .

I think I appreciate fully the objections to the law before us. But to deny that it presents a question upon which men might reasonably differ appears to me to be intolerance. And since men may so reasonably differ, I deem it beyond my constitutional power to assert my view of the wisdom of this law against the view of the State of West Virginia. [The Justice therefore holds, as he did in 1940, that a state has the right to require public school students to salute the flag.]

Religious Objections to War

The question of conscientious objection to military service is not a new problem in American history; indeed, it goes back to the American Revolution when Mennonites, Moravians, Quakers, and others found themselves unable, in good conscience, to bear arms. In Pennsylvania, for example, the Mennonites in 1775 petitioned that colony's General Assembly that they not be required to serve in a military capacity, "it being our principle to feed the hungry and give the thirsty drink." They added that they were dedicated to the idea of preserving life, not destroying it, and "we beg the patience of all those who believe we err in this point." During the Civil War and World War I and World War II, many conscientious objectors took their stand against war.

The problem for the nation became more acute, however, when many citizens who were not members of churches whose doctrine opposed bearing arms took an individual stand against a particular war, such as the war in Viet Nam. In the Universal Military Training and Service Act of 1948, Congress allowed for conscientious objection only on the basis of "religious training and belief." In a Supreme Court case in 1965, however, the Court indicated that any "sincere belief," whether explicitly religious or not, might provide a basis for exemption from the draft. Five years later, the Supreme Court divided on the question of whether views that were "essentially political, sociological, or philosophical" could become a valid ground for being excused from military duty. And in 1971, the Supreme Court decided that objection to a particular war rather than to all war in general was more likely to be based on political considerations than on religious conscience. As you read the excerpt below from *Gillette* v. *United States*, consider the following questions.

1. In your opinion, is allowing conscientious objectors the chance to do some other public service (clearing the forests, building roads, etc.) in place of military service a good idea or a bad one. Why?
2. Can you think of any situation in which you might consider some war in which your country is involved as being good, but some other war as being bad? Explain your response.
3. What does *capriciously* mean?

Gillette v. United States (1971)

The majority opinion was delivered by Mr. Justice Marshall.

. . . it is not unreasonable to suppose that some persons who are *not* prepared to assert a conscientious objection . . . may well agree at all

In the early 1980s, Enten Eller (shown here with Anna Mow) took a stand as a conscientious objector to war. Eller was a member of the Church of the Brethren, one of the "historic peace churches."

points with the objector, yet conclude, as a matter of conscience, that they are personally bound by the decision of the democratic process. The fear of the National Advisory Commission on Selective Service, apparently, is that exemption of objectors to particular wars would weaken the resolves of those who otherwise would feel themselves bound to serve despite personal cost, uneasiness at the prospect of violence, or even serious moral reservations or policy objections concerning the particular conflict.

. . . it is not inconsistent with orderly democratic government for individuals to be exempted by law, on account of special characteristics, from general duties of a burdensome nature. But real dangers . . . might arise if an exemption were made available that in its nature could not be administered fairly and uniformly. . . . Should it be thought that those who go to war are chosen unfairly or capriciously, then a mood of bitterness and cynicism might corrode the spirit of public service and the values of willing performance of a citizen's duties that are the very heart of free government.[9]

9 *Supreme Court Reporter,* Vol. 91, p. 841.

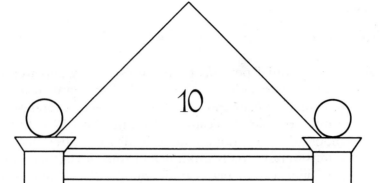

10

America:
Protestant
or Pluralist?

INTRODUCTION

PROTESTANT NATIVISM
AND ROMAN CATHOLIC
RESPONSE

ROMAN CATHOLICISM
AND ITS AMERICAN VARIETIES

JEWS IN AMERICA

EASTERN ORTHODOXY
IN AMERICA

THE ORIENT IN AMERICA

PATTERNS OF PLURALISM

PROBLEMS OF PLURALISM

Introduction

Throughout the colonial period of America's history and well into the nineteenth century, the nation was primarily Protestant in its religious make-up. To be more specific, Roman Catholics were a modest minority in America until a couple of decades before the Civil War. Judaism was even more modest in size until a couple of decades after that war. The Oriental religions were virtually unknown in America at that time. These very broad comments can be better understood with the help of the table below.

As you examine Table I determine the following and be prepared to discuss your findings:

1. Which groups seemed dominant in 1740? 1780? 1820?
2. Which groups seemed to grow most rapidly?
3. Offer some possible reasons why one group may grow more rapidly than another.

TABLE I

Number of Churches in America—1740, 1780, 1820

	1740	1780	1820
Anglican (Episcopal)	246	406	600
Baptist	96	457	2,700
Congregational	423	749	1,100
Dutch and German Reformed	129	328	480
Lutheran	95	240	800
Methodist	——	——	2,700
Presbyterian	160	495	1,700
Roman Catholic	27	56	124

In this same period, the total number of Jews in America was very tiny: about 1,100 in 1780, around 4,000 in 1820. The number of synagogues was so small at the end of the colonial period that they can be listed individually. There were five located in the following cities: New

York; Newport, Rhode Island; Savannah, Georgia; Charleston, South Carolina; and Philadelphia.

It should be apparent, therefore, that Protestantism held a prominent and relatively secure position in the earlier years of our national history. By 1850, however, Roman Catholicism had become the largest single denomination in the United States—a position of leadership that it still retains. And by 1950, the number in Jews in America had increased from the tiny fraction of colonial times to more than five million.

During the years of Judaism's rapid growth, another religious family, Eastern Orthodoxy, came in greater number to America. Eastern Orthodox churches were Catholic but not *Roman* Catholic. These Eastern Catholics did not accept the unique authority of the Pope, the Bishop of Rome. Rather, such persons as the Patriarch[1] of Constantinople or the Patriarch of Moscow were honored as the leading ecclesiastical authorities. Eastern Orthodox Christians are divided into many national groups (Russian, Greek, Bulgarian, Syrian, Serbian, and others); yet they share some similarities in creed and in the nature of their worship. Numbering only about 100,000 at the beginning of the twentieth century, Eastern Orthodoxy in America had grown by the 1980s to between three and four million adherents. By that time, the nation had also become host to many religions other than Judaism and Christianity, such as Hinduism, Buddhism, and Islam. The pathways to pluralism had broadened, and religious diversity was more and more a mark of the United States.

How did Protestants react to the shifting religious patterns that resulted in the loss of their religious monopoly? How did newer religious groups adjust to the American environment, to America's separation of church and state, to religious competition, and religious variety? These are questions that will be examined in this chapter. What tensions or problems does pluralism present to the society and to the nation? This most important question is one that will concern you as a citizen for years to come.

Protestant Nativism and Roman Catholic Response

Nativism refers to the fear of the foreign and excessive pride in what is already familiarly native—in this case, American. Of course, not all

---

1 *Patriarch*—literally, a "father ruler"; in Eastern Orthodoxy, the highest ranking bishops; bishops either of the major cities (Constantinople, Alexandria, Moscow, etc.) or of the major branches within Orthodoxy (Albanian, Bulgarian, Serbian, etc.).

nativism is motivated by or directed against religion. But in nineteenth-century America, the older inhabitants tended to be Protestant while the newer immigrants tended to be Catholic or Jewish or Eastern Orthodox. Thus, fear of the foreign and resentment against the immigrant often took on a religious aspect.

The campaigns against Catholicism were blatant and on occasion violent. In Massachusetts in 1834, an Ursuline convent was burned to the ground by local workmen angered by the competition of cheap Irish Catholic labor. A decade later, riots in Philadelphia resulted in the destruction of two Catholic churches, the killing of thirteen citizens, and the wounding of more than fifty. Nativism, then, was more than a mere sentiment; it was a threat to the democratic structure and constitutional ideals of the nation as a whole.

As you read about nativism and the Catholic response to it, think about the following. Be prepared to discuss the questions after reading all of this section.

1. According to the advice of the bishops, how should Catholics react to attacks by nativists? Was this good advice? Why or why not? How do you feel Catholics could best answer the false charges leveled against them?
2. Which of four points of Article II of the Constitution of the American Protective Association do you consider the least defensible as legitimate church goals? Why? Are any defensible? If so, which? Why?
3. Examine the points used by Josiah Strong to illustrate the claim that Catholicism and the Republic were incompatible. Explain your choices.
   a. Which would be easiest to refute?
   b. Which would be the most difficult to refute?
   c. Are there any that need no refutation?
4. What is the main theme of Cardinal Gibbons? Is this a good way of opposing the nativists?
5. What evidence can you find in the four readings that the charges against Catholics had changed little from 1833 to 1909? Are any of these charges leveled at Catholics today?

Pastoral letter, 1833[2]

As early as 1833, Roman Catholic bishops in America took public notice of the growing hostility of their Protestant neighbors.

The Roman Catholic Cathedral of Santa Fe, New Mexico, stands as the historic center of Hispanic Catholicism in the United States.

We notice with regret a spirit exhibited in the press which has within a few years become more unkind and unjust in our regard. Not only do they [Protestant supporters] assail us and our institutions in a style of abuse and condemnation, but they also misrepresent our doctrines, attack our practices and repeat the old false charges against the Catholic Church which have been refuted a hundred times. Moreover, they have denounced all of us as enemies to the liberties of the republic and have openly declared the fancied necessity of not only obstructing our progress but of using their best efforts to destroy our religion. . . .

We are too well known to our fellow citizens to make it necessary for us to show how groundless these charges are. We therefore advise you [members of the Catholic Church] to pay no attention to these attacks. Rather, we urge you to continue, while serving God faithfully, to discharge honestly, faithfully and with affection your duties to the government under which you live. In this way, we may with our fellow-citizens maintain this nation built on rational liberty in which we find such excellent protection.

American Protective Association

Nativism, to be effective, required organization. In 1842, the American Protective Association was formed in Philadelphia—two years before the bloody riots broke out in that city. The Association's purposes were clearly anti-Catholic, as its constitution indicates.[3] "Popery" and "Romanism"

2 Adapted from Peter Guilday, *The National Pastorals of the American Hierarchy, 1790–1919*, Washington, 1923 (reprinted by The Newman Press, Westminster, Md., 1954), p.78.

3 John Tracy Ellis, *Documents of American Catholic History* (Milwaukee: Bruce Publishing Co., 1962), p. 264.

were terms commonly used in the nineteenth century by those outside
the Roman Catholic church.

> Whereas, we believe the system of Popery to be, in its principles and
> tendency, subversive of civil and religious liberty, and destructive to
> the spiritual welfare of men, we unite for the purpose of defending
> our Protestant interests against the great exertions now making to
> propagate that system in the United States; and adopt the following
> constitution:—

> Article I. This Society shall be called the American Protective As-
> sociation.
> Article II. The objects of its formation, and for the attainment of
> which its efforts shall be directed are—
> 1. The union and encouragement of Protestant ministers of the
>   gospel, to give to their several congregations instruction on the
>   differences between Protestantism and Popery.
> 2. To call attention to the necessity of a more extensive distribution,
>   and thorough study of the Holy Scriptures.
> 3. The circulation of books and tracts adapted to give information
>   on the various errors of Popery in their history, tendency, and
>   design.
> 4. To awaken the attention of the community to the dangers which
>   threaten the liberties, and the public and domestic institutions,
>   of these United States from the assaults of Romanism.
> Article III. This Association shall be composed of all such persons
> as agree in adopting the purposes and principles of this constitution
> and contribute to the funds by which it is supported. . . .

A Debate

During and just after the Civil War, nativist attitudes that were earlier
found, for example, in the Know-Nothing or American Party declined.
In the 1880s resistance to increased immigration arose once more. Rumors
spread about papal plots to "make America Catholic," to destroy the American system of public education, to weaken or dissolve the separation
between church and state. Around the turn of the century, the debate
grew to major proportions. The violence of the earlier period was not
repeated, but some of the sentiments were. At a dignified level of discussion—represented here by the Reverend Josiah Strong (Congregationalist) and by James Cardinal Gibbons (Roman Catholic)—the sharp divisions
of opinion still appeared.

Josiah Strong in 1891 published an important volume, *Our Country: Its Possible Future and Its Present Crisis.* In this book, Strong argued for a preservation of the Anglo-Saxon Protestant heritage, even as he pointed out the "perils of Romanism."

We have made a brief comparison of some of the fundamental principles of Romanism with those of the Republic. And,

1. We have seen the supreme sovereignty of the Pope opposed to the sovereignty of the people.
2. We have seen that the commands of the Pope, instead of the constitution and the law of the land, demand the highest allegiance of Roman Catholics in the United States.
3. We have seen that the alien Romanist who seeks citizenship swears true obedience to the Pope instead of "renouncing forever all allegiance to any foreign prince, potentate, state or sovereignty," as required by our laws.
4. We have seen that Romanism teaches religious intolerance instead of religious liberty.
5. We have seen that Rome demands the censorship of ideas and of the press, instead of the freedom of the press and of speech.
6. We have seen that she approves the union of church and state instead of their entire separation.
7. We have seen that she is opposed to our public school system.

Manifestly there is an irreconcilable difference between papal principles and the fundamental principles of our free institutions. Popular government is self-government. A nation is capable of self-government only so far as the individuals who compose it are capable of self-government. To place one's conscience, therefore, in the keeping of another, and to disavow all personal responsibility in obeying the dictation of another, is as far as possible from *self*-government. It is the theory of absolutism in the state, that man exists for the state. It is the theory of absolutism in the church that man exists for the church. But in republican and Protestant America it is believed that church and state exist for the people and are to be administered by them. Our fundamental ideas of society, therefore, are as radically opposed to Vaticanism as to imperialism, and it is as inconsistent with our liberties for Americans to yield allegiance to the Pope as to the Czar.

Many of our Roman Catholic fellow citizens undoubtedly love the country, and believe that in seeking to Romanize it they are serving its highest interests. But when we remember, as has been shown, that the fundamental principles of Romanism are opposed to those of the

159

Republic, that the difference between them does not admit of adjustment, but is diametric and utter, it becomes evident that it would be impossible to "make America Catholic," without bringing the principles of that church into active conflict with those of our government. Thus Roman Catholics would be compelled to choose between them. In that event, every Romanist who remained obedient to the Pope, that is, who continued to be Romanist, would necessarily become disloyal to our free institutions.

Responding to these and like charges, Cardinal Gibbons, Archbishop of Baltimore, wrote an essay on "The Church and the Republic."[5]

Sixteen millions of Catholics live their lives on our land with undisturbed belief in the perfect harmony existing between their religion and their duties as American citizens. It never occurs to their minds to question the truth of a belief which all their experience confirms. Love of religion and love of country burn together in their hearts.

They love their Church as the divine spiritual society set up by Jesus Christ, through which they are brought into a closer communion with God, learn His revealed truth and His holy law, receive the help they need to lead Christian lives, and are inspired with the hope of eternal happiness. They love their country with the spontaneous and ardent love of all patriots, because it is their country, and the source to them of untold blessings. They prefer its form of government before any other. They admire its institutions and the spirit of its laws. They accept the Constitution without reserve, with no desire, as Catholics, to see it changed in any feature. They can, with a clear conscience, swear to uphold it. . . .

Two synods[6] of Protestant ministers have deemed it just and wise to proclaim to the country that Catholics cannot be trusted with political office; that they cannot sincerely subscribe to the Federal Constitution; that their loyalty is illogical, being contradictory to the teachings of the Church; that their religion is opposed to American liberties; and that they themselves, kept in the dark by their religious guides, are ignorant of the true nature of their Church's doctrines. In sounding forth these charges to American Catholics, and to the country in general, they declare themselves inspired, not by religious antagonism or the desire

5 This essay appeared in the *North American Review* (vol. 189) in March of 1909. It was also included in the Cardinal's autobiography, *A Retrospect of Fifty Years* (Baltimore and New York, John Murphy & Co., 1916), vol. I, p. 216.

6 *Synod*—an assembly of presbyteries; an ecclesiastical council.

In 1961 the nation's first Roman Catholic president, John F. Kennedy, took the oath of office as the thirty-fifth president.

to profit by a good opportunity, but solely by patriotic solicitude for the permanence of American institutions. . . .

The Catholic religion, as they understand it, is in conflict with the Federal Constitution, and with the object of our institutions; Catholics, then, ought not to be trusted with political office. Accordingly, Americans should seek to exclude Catholics from the chair of the President, who is called upon to enforce the Constitution; from the Supreme Bench, whose duty it is to interpret it; from the Senate and the Houses of Representatives, which have the power to change it. And as the chief evil dreaded from Catholics is a modification of the existing relations between Church and State, a power theoretically reserved to our State Governments, no Catholic should be chosen Governor, State legislator or judge of a supreme State Court. This is the scope of their meaning, though not all explicitly avowed. It would logically be desirable to deny Catholics the right to vote, and with men in the frame of mind their attitude suggests, the realization of this desire in the statute books, and of their complete program, would only be a matter of their possessing sufficient power and judging the act politically expedient.

Now this proposal to exclude Catholics from office—for it is no mere theory, but a practical program earnestly recommended to the American public by two solemn assemblies—is advocated expressly in the interest of religious liberty and for the sake of preserving

Federal Constitution. That document says: "no religious test shall ever be required as a qualification to any office or public trust under the United States." Just understand here, however, remark these Lutheran and Baptist synods, an amendment, or rather let us say, a little clause which brings out the sense with admirable clearness: "Provided, of course, that this provision be not understood to apply to Roman Catholics."

Such restrictions on religion have always been felt to be incompatible with American ideas, and have fallen, though sometimes only after a long struggle, before the force of the real American spirit. . . .

There must be no tampering with the delicate machinery by which religious liberty and equality are secured, and no fostering of any spirit which would tend to destroy that machinery. Religious passions are deep and strong; and any man in his senses who knows human nature or knows the history of Europe, and has at heart the future peace and happiness of our country, whatever his belief, will do nothing to introduce religious strife into the politics of America. Religious tolerance is not the easy superficial virtue it seems in these placid days; intolerance in the dominating party tends to produce intolerance in the injured party. Then religious peace is near an end, unless strong restraints be used. The spirit of the country has changed much in half a century, and it would be very difficult to arouse such fanaticism as I saw in the Know-Nothing days. Prudent men, men who are farsighted, especially if they are in positions of responsibility, will work for peace and harmony.

Roman Catholicism and Its American Varieties

When the Roman Catholic church became the nation's largest denomination shortly before the Civil War, the largest ethnic component of that church was Irish. Fleeing from the poverty and hunger of their native land, thousands (and by 1850 the number had grown to a million) left Ireland for the promise of a better life in America. As the largest body of English-speaking Catholics, the Irish moved readily into roles of leadership in Eastern cities and in the Roman Catholic Church. Soon the hierarchy of this large church in America grew to be mainly Irish.

At times there were difficulties with other immigrant groups who were Catholic but emphatically not Irish. A Milwaukee priest, writing on behalf of German Catholics in 1886, argued that it made most sense for German congregations to have German priests and even German bishops.

Mexican-Americans celebrate the mass in the Roman Catholic tradition.

It was not so much a matter of language, he noted, as of difference in social customs, in ceremonies and processions, in feasts and saints days, and even in parish administration. So many differences exist between the Irish and the Germans that one will scarcely ever "find Germans and Irish united in matrimony," the Milwaukee priest noted. Polish Catholics and later Italian Catholics also argued for more attention to their own ethnic and national differences, a minority of the Poles even going so far as to organize in 1904 the Polish National Catholic Church. For the most part, however, the Roman Catholic Church in America managed to hold together those immigrants from widely separated lands, speaking many different languages, and observing greatly differing customs both in the churches and out.

Hispanic Catholics

In the twentieth century, the largest immigration of Roman Catholics to the United States came not from Europe but from Central and South America and Puerto Rico. As a result of this immigration, about one fourth of all Roman Catholics in America by the 1980s were of Hispanic descent. Yet, not until 1970 did the Church appoint its first Hispanic bishop, and not until 1972 did it hold a conference, or encuentro, that gave recognition to the large and largely ignored minority within the Roman Catholic Church. At the second National Pastoral Hispanic Conference, held in Washington, D.C., in 1977, Cuban bishop E.B. Masvidal, exiled from his own land, explained to those present how much the Hispanic population could give to the culture of the United States, and in turn how much the United States could offer to these newer citizens. Bishop Masvidal also spoke of the necessity to create "unity in pluralism," a challenge not just for the Roman Catholic church alone, but the nation as a whole.

> The Second National Hispanic Pastoral Encuentro, which has called together representatives from the various Hispanic communities residing in the United States, does not seek to isolate Hispanics from the mainstream, neither does it seek to encourage mistaken ideas of nationalism. Its objective, rather, is to accomplish the opposite: to create unity in pluralism and thereby to bear witness to the marvelous plan by which God made us all brothers, members of the large human family which is subject to His universal fatherhood. However, at the same time, He has made us all different, each with our own physical and spiritual identity.
>
> God, in His infinite wisdom, did not ordain that each of us be a "standard type," each cut with the same mold, uniform. He willed that individuals as well as nations retain their own identity, their language, their values, their customs, their history, their qualities and also their defects, that is to say, all those aspects which constitute their culture. Thus, even among the Hispanic nations, there exists a great deal of diversity. This diversity neither destroys nor does it go contrary to the unity which God intended for mankind, because unity is different from uniformity. It is compatible with the diversity in the same manner that each member of a family has his own personality. This in no way destroys the unity of the family. Yet, no member can take upon himself the right of absorbing another so as to make of the other a replica of himself.
>
> Great enrichment is possible whenever two cultures come together in a spirit of mutual respect, each contributing some of its values. This constitutes a healthy integration, and both benefit. However, the opposite occurs whenever one culture absorbs the other, because the assimilated culture has lost its own identity and its values. It is no longer itself. It is dead. . . .
>
> This unity in pluralism must be lived at many different levels. It must exist, first of all, within the Church. The Church is one and the

same throughout the world. Wherever we go, the bishop of that diocese becomes our pastor. We must feel that the local Church is our own. In his letter to the Ephesians, St. Paul enunciates the fundamental reasons for our unity: we all have "but one Lord, one faith, one baptism, one God and Father." . . .

Secondly, this unity in pluralism must be visible in the Church's attitude toward the exterior world. It must be open to all peoples of the world, to their anxieties and to their problems. In this same letter to the Ephesians, St. Paul tells us that Christ, by means of his death, tore down the wall of hatred which separated men, that He came to draw close all those who were far away from God. . . .

Today, more than ever, Christians must reject the temptation to isolate themselves in closed groups. If Christ called us to be "leaven," we have to be in the midst of all. Nevertheless, we must continue to be different, so that instead of adopting the principles and criteria of the world, we will be able to infuse it with Christian values. Our pluralism is not a confusion of ideas. It is not apathy, neither is it moral relativism. Our criteria and ideas must be very clearly delineated in our minds, even while we respect those held by others. Only in this way will our light shine before all men, so that they in turn will give glory to our Father in Heaven.[7]

Jews in America

Before the Civil War, Jews came to America chiefly from Germany. Afterwards, particularly in the final decades of the nineteenth century, the vast majority of Jews came from eastern European countries such as Russia, Rumania, and Poland. Jews faced many of the same nativist reactions confronted by Catholics. In addition, however, they were troubled by the differences and disagreements among themselves about adjustments and accommodations in America.

Many of the German Jews had been engaged in western European reform movements. Many were products of the European Enlightenment, were well educated, and were in close touch with the surrounding culture. These Jews had emerged from that ghetto in which they had for so long been confined. Eastern European Jews, on the other hand, had enjoyed little opportunity for broad cultural contacts and had little reason to trust

7 *Proceedings of the Segundo Encuentro Nacional Hispano de Pastoral*, (Washington, D.C., 1978), pp. 58-59.

or seek accommodation with the non-Jewish world. Persecution and social ostracism had been their lot. It was inevitable, therefore, that differences would arise among Jews themselves as well as with their new Gentile neighbors.

The German Jews formed the nucleus of Reform Judaism. This more liberal strain introduced many novel elements into synagogue life: use of the organ and mixed choirs, seating by families instead of separation by sex, translation of many prayers from Hebrew into English. Also the place of the Jewish law—the Torah—in the life of the Reform Jew was greatly modified. Food laws, ritual requirements in the home or synagogue, and many other details of daily behavior became optional rather than mandatory. Leaders in Reform Judaism also showed interest in becoming Americanized as rapidly as possible.

The Jews from eastern Europe formed the nucleus of Orthodox Judaism in America. In a strange land that practiced strange ways and spoke a strange tongue, these immigrants held tightly to that which was familiar and sacred. What other Jews might call reform many of these Jews would see as abandonment—a turning away from "the religion of Abraham, Isaac, and Jacob." In tightly knit communities, especially in and around New York City, Orthodox Judaism maintained a careful allegiance to the Mosaic Law. This included observing certain dietary laws (for example, eating only kosher[8] foods), preserving distinctive fashions of dress, maintaining Hebrew schools, avoiding intermarriage, and the like.

Between Reform on the one hand and Orthodoxy on the other, a third group, Conservative Judaism, developed. Reacting against too rapid a change by Reform Jews and at the same time rejecting the legalistic strictness of Orthodoxy, the Conservative Jews founded an important school in New York in 1885: the Jewish Theological Seminary. From that training center, the program of Conservative Judaism spread to many suburban areas around the country.

In the first section, we shall look at differences between two respected Jewish leaders in their understanding of how much Americanization among Jews is necessary or desirable. The second section treats the relationship between Jew and non-Jew in America, a relationship that depends primarily, of course, on the attitudes of the Gentile majority.

As you read about Americanization, think about the following. Be prepared to discuss the questions after reading the second section.

1. According to Rabbi Wise, why must a Jew become an American?

---

8 *Kosher*—fit, right, or proper; more specifically, food fit to eat according to Jewish law (see Leviticus 11).

On Ellis Island, October, 1912, immigrants to America await permission to begin a new life in the United States.

2. What might a German Jewish immigrant do to become Americanized?
3. As Rabbi Schechter speaks of the Jews' "glorious heritage" and the Torah, he reveals his concern with Americanization. To what is he primarily opposed?
4. What place, says Schechter, should the institution and laws of Judaism hold?
5. What had nativists implied that Catholics should give up? Could you say, then, that Jews and Catholics were being asked to pay the same price for Americanization? If so, what was it?

Americanization

Rabbi Isaac M. Wise (1819–1900), a German Jew and the most significant of the early reforming rabbis in America, served principally in Cincinnati, where in 1875 he opened the Hebrew Union College. In his *Reminiscences* (first published in 1874), he offered his thoughts on Americanizing.

> The Jew must be Americanized, I said to myself, for every German book, every German word reminds him of the old disgrace. If he continues under German influences, as they are now in this country, he must become either a bigot or an atheist, a satellite or tyrant. He will

never be aroused to self-consciousness or to independent thought. The Jew must become an American, in order to gain the proud self-consciousness of the free-born man.

From that hour I began to Americanize with all my might and was as enthusiastic for this as I was for Reform.

Solomon Schechter (1847–1915), a noted biblical scholar, was an eastern European Jew. In 1902 he became president of Jewish Theological Seminary in New York. His views below are adapted from a 1904 address printed in *Seminary Addresses and Other Papers* (Cincinnati, 1915).

There is nothing in American Citizenship which is incompatible with our keeping the Sabbath holy, our fixing a Mezuzah[9] on our doorposts, our refraining from unleavened[10] bread on Passover,[11] or our keeping any other law essential to the preservation of Judaism. On the other hand, it is now generally recognized that the institutions and observances of religion are part of its [essential] nature. This fact the "enlightened" rationalism of a half century ago failed to realize. In certain parts of Europe every step in our civil and social emancipation demanded from us a corresponding sacrifice of a portion of the glorious heritage bequeathed to us by our fathers. Jews in America, thank God, are no longer haunted by such fears. We live in a commonwealth in which by the blessing of God and the wisdom of the Fathers of the Constitution, each man abiding by its laws, has the inalienable right of living in accordance with the dictates of his own conscience. In this great, glorious and free country we Jews need not sacrifice a single iota of our Torah; and, in the enjoyment of absolute equality with our fellow citizens, we can live to carry out those ideals for which our ancestors so often had to die.

Anti-Semitism

Like nativism, anti-Semitism is not necessarily motivated by or directed against a religion. Once again like nativism, however, anti-Semitism in America often placed the adherents of one religion—in this case, Chris-

---

9 *Mezuzah*—a small parchment scroll (with verses of Scripture on it), placed in a box and put outside the main door of the home as a sign of Jewish faith.

10 *Unleavened*—without yeast or baking soda.

11 *Passover*—The sacred meal commemorating the deliverance of the Jews from slavery in Egypt; observed in the home.

tianity—in opposition to the adherents to another religion—in this case, Judaism.

It is useful to remember that Judaism and Christianity have a parent-child relationship, for the early Christians were Jews and early Christianity could be viewed as a sect or division in first-century Judaism. But as the child broke away from the parental home, hostility often resulted. Jews were charged with having misunderstood their own Scripture, with having rejected the promised Messiah, and with being responsible for the crucifixion of Christ. By a curious and tragic logic, some Christians in later centuries held all Jews responsible for the death of Christ.

In the most important church council of modern times, Vatican II (1963–65), the Roman Catholic church sought to correct long standing anti-Semitic attitudes, especially those based on ecclesiastical grounds. One of the Church's documents, entitled "Declaration on the Relationship of the Church to Non-Christian Religions," spoke explicitly to this question. It argued that the suffering of Christ "cannot be blamed upon all Jews then living, without distinction, nor upon the Jews of today." The document further asserted that "The Church repudiates all persecutions against any man . . . she deplores the hatred, persecutions, and displays of anti-Semitism directed against the Jews at any time and from any source."[12]

Such sentiments, however noble, have not removed all the sources for or manifestations of hostility directed toward the Jew. As you read about anti-Semitism, consider the following questions and be prepared to discuss them.

1. Why is anti-Semitism fundamentally anti-Christian?
2. Rabbi Gilbert notes that anti-Semites allude to the threat of "Jewish bankers" and "Jewish Communists."
   a. If an anti-Semite warned against both of these, would his charge be self-contradictory? Why or why not?
   b. To whom might the "bankers" charge appeal? To whom might the "Communists" charge appeal?
3. Both religious and racial anti-Semitism are referred to. What do these modifiers mean? What other types might exist? To whom would these types appeal?
4. According to Gilbert's quote from H.A. Overstreet, of what are too many Americans guilty? Explain.
5. Following Overstreet's hints, how can Americans eliminate anti-Semitism?

12 See Walter M. Abbott, S.J. (ed.), *The Documents of Vatican II* (New York, 1966), p. 665-667.

Christians and Anti-Semitism

In 1964, an English translation of Jules Isaac's book *The Teaching of Contempt: Christian Roots of Anti-Semitism* was published in this country. It had originally appeared in France in 1962—the same year that Pope John XXIII convened the most important church council of modern times: Vatican Council II. Isaac, most of whose own family had been put to death by the German Gestapo, wished to trace or expose the sources for anti-Semitism that lay within Christianity itself. His brief foreword and a portion of the first chapter follow.[13]

We are all familiar with the words of Jesus from the Fourth Gospel, "In my Father's house are many mansions" (John 14:2). I fear that in Satan's house there are even more—if only to accommodate the thousand varieties of anti-Semitism whose most virulent form in our day would seem to be Hitler's racial anti-Semitism.

Need I apologize, then, for carrying on my struggle to expose— and, if possible, to extirpate—the Christian roots of anti-Semitism? No, for in my opinion they are the deepest ones of all.

I am told that I would do better to devote myself to some constructive task: rather than denounce the teaching of contempt, why not initiate the teaching of respect?

But the two ends are inseparable. It is impossible to combat the teaching of contempt and its modern survivals, without thereby laying the foundations for the teaching of respect; and, conversely, it is impossible to establish the teaching of respect, without first destroying the remnants of the teaching of contempt. Truth cannot be built upon error.

A work of purification is never a negative activity. For us, such an effort is an essential preliminary, which we shall never cease to recommend to every Christian conscience.

Preliminary Considerations

"There is something worse than having an evil mind, and that is having a closed one." —CHARLES PÉGUY

"It is a fundamental rule of life never to distort the truth." —POPE JOHN XXIII

---

13 From *The Teaching of Contempt,* by Jules Isaac, translated by Helen Weaver, copyright 1964 by Holt, Rinehart and Winston, Inc., reprinted by permission of the publisher.

All authorities are agreed that a true Christian cannot be an anti-Semite.

Let us begin by recalling that the term *anti-Semitism* is used nowadays to refer to anti-Jewish prejudice, to feelings of suspicion, contempt, hostility, and hatred toward Jews, both those who follow the religion of Israel and those who are merely of Jewish parentage.

Given this, here is my first statement of principle: All authorities are agreed that anti-Semitism is by definition unchristian, even anti-Christian. A true Christian cannot be an anti-Semite; he simply has no right to be one.

"The Church teaches that there is only one human race, and that by nature all men are and always will be brothers, not only by virtue of their common origin, but also for a still more exalted reason, the universal redemption of man, which Jesus Christ, through the operation of grace, accomplished by his death on the cross." This is why "anti-Semitism amounts to a form of anti-Christianity." (L.T. Devaux, Superior-General of the Missionary Priests of Our Lady of Zion)

"Anti-Semitic hatred is an anti-Christian madness which would render meaningless the martyrdom and death of Jesus." (Jacques Maritain)

The Protestants add their voices to those of the Catholics:

"Anti-Semitism is a sin against the Holy Ghost, because it implies the rejection of divine grace." (Karl Barth)

"We declare anti-Semitism to be a plain denial of the spirit of our Lord. A Christian cannot be anti-Semitic in thought, word, or deed without being unfaithful to his Christian heritage." (Statement of the Federal Council of Churches in America, 1938)

"We call upon all the churches we represent to denounce anti-Semitism, no matter what its origin, as absolutely irreconcilable with the profession and practice of the Christian faith. Anti-Semitism is sin against God and man." (Resolution of the World Council of Churches, Amsterdam, 1948)

Americans and Anti-Semitism

The Anti-Defamation League of B'nai B'rith, organized in America in 1913, arose (as its name implies) to put down the rumors and set aside the character assassinations that were again and again directed against Jews or against any others. The former director of the Religious Curriculum Research Department of that League, Rabbi Arthur Gilbert (1926–1976), shows how necessary such vigilant defense always is. One chapter of his book *A Jew in Christian America*[14] reviews anti-Semitism in this country. It is a symbol of a pluralist America that this essay, written by a rabbi, first appeared in a Protestant journal and was then included in a book published by a Catholic press.

> The period between 1881–1914 was a time of mass migration and industrial expansion and 22,000,000 migrants of every religious persuasion, chiefly from Eastern and Southern Europe, rushed through "the Golden Door."
>
> Emma Lazarus, a German Jewish poet, was so moved by America's hospitality, that in 1883 she composed her sonnet "The New Colossus," whose immortal words were later to be inscribed on the Statue of Liberty. She sang:

> > *. . . Give me your tired, your poor,*
> > *Your huddled masses yearning to breathe free,*
> > *The wretched refuse of your teeming shore,*
> > *Send these, the homeless, tempest-tossed, to me.*

Two million Jews accepted this invitation and, indeed, for them America was a golden land. No other ethnic or religious group can boast the same rapid climb up the ladder of cultural, economic, and social success. It was exactly this rapid advancement of the Jew, however, that provided the occasion for a new form of social discrimination in the United States. . . .

Thus, once again, the paradox. Even as America gave with one hand, there were some who would take away with the other.

Anti-Semitic agitators, Protestant nativists, the socially insecure, and even fearful liberals in the Labor Movement joined forces to close the door to immigration. In 1924 Congress adopted a shameful racist immigration bill.

From the World War I period on until the adoption of the Johnson Immigration Measure, America had witnessed a continual harangue of anti-foreign, anti-Semitic, anti-Catholic, and anti-Negro hatred. The address of Imperial Wizard Evans, before 75,000 Klansmen in Dallas, Texas, October 24, 1923, is representative: "Negroes, Catholics, and Jews," Evans asserted, "are the undesirable elements in America, defying every fundamental requirement of assimilation. They are incapable of attaining the Anglo-Saxon level." Jews were specifically accused of being an "absolutely unblendable element" for whom "patriotism as the

---

14 *A Jew in Christian America* by Rabbi Arthur Gilbert, ©Sheed and Ward, Inc., 1966.

Anglo-Saxon feels it, is impossible.". . .

Inevitably the participation of some Jews in the Bolshevik revolution and then the depression of 1929 provided anti-Semites with all the evidence that they needed to step up their claim that "Jewish bankers" or "Jewish Communists" were involved in a world-wide financial manipulation or revolution, the exact charge depending, of course, on the bigot and the gullibility of his audience. Even the halls of Congress echoed with such charges. . . .

Hitler's rise to power in Germany had its serious repercussions in the United States. As the House un-American Affairs Committee has revealed, hundreds of anti-Jewish organizations bounded into existence. The Committee listed 135 of them. They were not insignificant. Fritz Kuhn's "German-American Bund" claimed a membership of 25,000. Its Madison Square rally was attended by 19,000 and from the rafters a sign shouted: "Wake Up America. Smash Jewish Communism. Stop Jewish Domination of Christian America.". . .

No wonder, then, that the Jewish community expanded the work of defense agencies such as the Anti-Defamation League, the American-Jewish Committee, and the American-Jewish Congress.

With the end of World War II, however, America entered a new era. The Jews had demonstrated their allegiance with their blood. Americans realized the bitter price civilization must pay for hatred allowed to run rampant. Without question, a resolve was evident nationwide that once and for all discrimination should be buried in this land.

The national effort to end racial segregation is evidence of this resolve in action. Yet again, hatemongers and right wing extremists are at work. Some of these are the same Nazis and anti-Semites who were in operation prior to World War II. Their newspapers cry out the alarm that the Civil Rights Movement is allegedly under the domination of Zionist-Communists. The National Council of Churches, it is claimed, has sold out to the Jews, and America itself is in danger of subversion from within. . . .

Jewish community relations agencies reveal that anti-Semitism is now at its lowest point, particularly in those areas where they have devoted their major educational energies. In the most recent 20-year period, restrictive quotas on admission of Jews in professional schools has almost been eliminated and resort hotel discrimination is virtually extinct. Unlike a former period, the use of anti-Semitism in a political campaign today is sure to doom the candidate to failure.

Yet recent surveys reveal also that 72% of private clubs and 60% of city clubs still discriminate on grounds of religion. Jews are still barred from upper echelon positions in banking, insurance, and in the best law firms. They are still denied housing in the most exclusive communities. 32% of Americans in 1960 confessed that they were uncertain or would not vote for a president nominated by their own political party if he were a Jew, even if he were well qualified. Jews cannot forget so easily that just five years ago, in 1960, during the German swastika epidemic, there were also 700 incidents of anti-Jewish desecration reported in the United States over an eight-week period.

It appears to me that the time is now for Americans to end such nonsense. "What ye do to the least of these, ye do to me."

It is also well here to recall Henry A. Overstreet's warning that the main problem stems not from those who impose restrictions against Jews, but from those who acquiesce to them. Said Overstreet:

He who permits evil, commits evil. This is what makes for the haunting sense of guilt in our culture. Many a member of the dominant group will earnestly aver that *he* never intended that Negroes should be insulted and maltreated . . . that *his heart* is sore and ashamed when he reads of the defiling of Jewish synagogues by hoodlums. He did not intend these things, but *he created the social sanction for these things.* By adopting a twisted principle of human association, he and the people like him open the Pandora's box out of which have flown the intolerance and cruelties that have defiled our culture.

Jews and Judaism

One of the permanently difficult questions in human history sounds all too simple: Who is a Jew? Jewish scholars are themselves divided in their responses, for the question involves intricate matters of race and religion, of ethnic identity and political loyalty. A less complicated question—at least on first glance—is this: What is Judaism? The answer would appear to be simple, "It is the religion of the Jews." And this would apparently escape all difficulty of defining a "Jew." But only apparently, for in another form the complexities remain. In what ways may a Jew be "religious"? Is the Jew's religion more a matter of behavior or of belief: is Judaism also a history and a civilization as well as a synagogue and a denomination?

Mordecai Kaplan (1881–1983), the founder of a movement known as Reconstructionism, argued that Jews were not so much a church as they were a people. Judaism was not so much a religion as it was a religious civilization. As one scholar has written, "Kaplan provided a rationale for those Jews who no longer believed in the divine origin of Jewish religious law but who nevertheless wanted to keep on living as Jews."[15] Kaplan's two major works are *Judaism as a Civilization*, published in 1934, and *The Future of an American Jew*, published in 1949. The following selection[16] is adapted from the second book (pp. xviif., 35-36, 56-57). As you read Kaplan's words, consider the following questions:

1. How do you understand the expression "religious civilization"?
2. What three contemporary problems does Kaplan hope to solve for American Jews?
3. Judging from the passage given here, what are some of the "universal human values" you would expect Kaplan to support?

The basic premise of the Reconstructionist Movement is that Judaism is not merely a religion but a religious civilization. Accordingly, the decisive factor in the present inner crisis of Jewish life is the Jew's necessity to live in two civilizations. These are Judaism and Americanism in this country, or Judaism and some other modern civilization elsewhere.

*   *   *

It is certainly not true that religion, or a particular set of beliefs about God, with practices related to these beliefs, is all that distinguishes the Jews as a group from non-Jews. If Judaism is to mean that which unites Jews into an identifiable and distinct group, then it is a religious civilization. As such, Judaism is the ensemble of the following interrelated elements of culture: a feeling of belonging to a historic and indivisible people, rootage in a common land, a continuing history, a living language and literature, and common mores, laws and arts, with religion as the integrating and soul-giving factor of all those elements.

The peoplehood, the culture and the religion of the Jews are one and inseparable. Their mutual relationship may be compared to that which exists among the three dimensions of physical body. They correspond to the three concepts referred to in the popular dictum: *Israel, the Torah and the Holy One, blessed be He, are one.* In this statement, "Israel" represents peoplehood; "Torah," or Israel's way of life, represents culture; and "The Holy One" represents religion. The purpose in pronouncing them one is to stress the fact that none of the three terms can even be understood except in relation to the other two. Jewish religion, Jewish peoplehood and Jewish culture are all aspects of the same reality, and each is meaningless apart from its relation to the totality of Jewish life.

In the light of that conception of Judaism and of the contemporary

15 Nathan Glazer, *American Judaism* (Chicago: University of Chicago Press, 1957), p. 97.

16 Mordecai Kaplan, *The Future of An American Jew* (New York: Jewish Reconstructionist Press, 1945). Reprinted with permission of Hebrew Publishing Company.

inner and outer challenge to Jewish life, the problem we have on our hands reduces itself to the following questions:

In the first place, what has to be done, socially and culturally, to enable the present generation of Jews to feel its oneness with all the preceding generations of the Jewish people?

Secondly, how shall we reinterpret our tradition, so that it can be rendered compatible with a reasonable conception of naturalism and an ethical conception of nationalism?

Thirdly, how can we make room in Judaism for diversity of world outlook and religious practice, and have as the test of Jewish loyalty mainly the sincere desire to have Jewish life survive, grow and exert a [healthy] influence on human life in general?

The reconstruction of Jewish life and thought will thus have to consist in the pursuit of the following objectives:

1. The rebuilding of [the State of Israel] as the creative center of Judaism.
2. The creation of an adequate social structure for democratic Jewish communal life in the [rest of the world].
3. The redirection of Jewish education to conform with the conception of Judaism as a religious civilization.
4. The revitalization of Jewish religion.
5. The stimulation of Jewish cultural creativity in literature and the arts.
6. The participation of Jewry in social movements that seek ampler freedom, stricter justice and better cooperation among men and nations.

*   *   *

Only a Judaism calculated to bring out all that is best in human nature, and to guide us Jews in applying that best to all our human interests, can command sufficient loyalty to insure its survival and advancement. America is a cultural melting pot. Cultural differences that do not contribute to the realization of universal human values are bound to vanish. It is generally recognized that all men need to be rooted in a religious tradition, and that it is to the various historic religions, older than America itself, that the American nation looks for the strengthening of its own morale. It looks to Judaism, and rightly so, to accomplish this for its Jewish citizens. That expectation is an unequally opportunity for us Jews not only to retain our group life in this country, but also to achieve a religious orientation that might prove of great value to the religiously starved mankind of our day. This is the unique chance which the God of history has given us; let us not fumble it.

A Greek Orthodox church in Sitka, Alaska, around 1900.

Eastern Orthodoxy in America

Roman Catholic emigration to America was, as we have seen, largely a feature of the mid-nineteenth century. Jewish emigration reached major proportions in the latter decades of that century. In the case of Eastern Orthodoxy, the great growth from abroad has been in the twentieth century. We would expect, therefore, that the problems of Americanization have come later for Orthodoxy than for Judaism and Roman Catholicism. Such is, in fact, the case.

Before looking at those problems, however, it would be well to get as clear a picture as we can of the many groups in America assumed under the title of *Orthodox*. This title is also an ordinary English word, of course, meaning "correct opinion." In religious terms, opinion that is incorrect may be called heresy, unorthodox, or heterodox, which literally means "other opinion." In ancient Christian history—especially the fourth through the sixth centuries—the title Orthodox distinguished the majority of Christendom from smaller groups that did not accept the creeds of such vital church councils as Nicea (A.D. 325) and Chalcedon (A.D. 451). These smaller groups were, then, heretical or heterodox.

One other item of earlier history must be noted before we come to the American scene. In the eleventh century, A.D. 1054 to be exact, the Eastern and Western branches of Christendom officially—and bitterly—separated from each other. Thus the modifier *Eastern* is placed before Orthodoxy to designate one half of this great separation or schism. The other half (instead of being called Western Orthodoxy, which would be quite logical) is designated Roman Catholicism. The modifier *Roman* indicates immediately a loyalty to the Bishop of Rome, the Pope, as a unique ecclesiastical authority. The term *catholic*, like *orthodox*, is an ancient one, used to distinguish the vast majority of early Christendom (*catholic* means "universal") from the smaller heretical or schismatic groups. Since the eleventh century, therefore, the Eastern and Western halves of ancient, pre-Reformation Christianity have been separated from each other.

The Eastern churches developed their organization chiefly along national lines. In each country, the Orthodox Church had its own structure and its leading bishop or Patriarch (father). Thus, in Syria or Rumania, Bulgaria or Greece, Albania or Russia, the Orthodox Church became the dominant religious institution. Now each of these in its own country was simply *the* Orthodox Church. But when in the twentieth century, members of these national churches came to the United States, distinguishing titles became necessary. The listing of the varied groups can, therefore, sound quite confusing: Albanian Orthodox Diocese of America, American Carpatho-Russian Orthodox Greek Catholic Diocese, Greek Orthodox Archdiocese of North and South America, Bulgarian Eastern Orthodox Church—and so on! It must also be confessed that like other churches in America some of these national groups have split among themselves, further complicating the picture.

We can simplify it a bit by recognizing that two national groups—the Russians and the Greeks—constitute the largest representatives of Eastern Orthodoxy in America. Russian Orthodox churches have an old tradition in North America, since they were established in Alaska as early as 1794 when that territory belonged to Czarist Russia. The major strength today of Russian Orthodoxy in America, however, is due to twentieth century immigration. As a result of this later immigration and of the 1917 political

Russian Orthodox worshippers gather in New York City early in the twentieth century.

revolution in Russia, there are now three Russian Orthodox groups in America: (1) the Russian Orthodox Greek Catholic Church of America,[17] the largest of the three; (2) the Russian Orthodox Church outside of Russia, which has about 80 churches in this country; and (3) the smallest of the three, the Russian Orthodox Church in the Americas, which maintains official connection with the "Patriarch of Moscow and of all Russia."

The Greek immigration to the United States had exceeded 100,000 by World War I. A second great wave of immigration followed World War II. By the end of the 1980s, well over two million Greek Catholics were to be found in the Greek Orthodox Archdiocese of North and South America.

How much adjustment to the American environment has Eastern Orthodoxy made? How much is desirable? How much is required? In the nineteenth century, one problem facing many immigrant groups was that of language. Was it necessary to learn English in order to be Americanized? While the answer to that question was generally yes, this did not mean that English had to become the language of the synagogue or church.

17 Granted its autonomy by the Moscow Patriarch in 1970.

Many churches, therefore, maintained German or Polish or Danish or Hebrew or Greek long after English had become the common tongue apart from worship. So also with Eastern Orthodoxy where the use of English in worship or in church publications or even in theological discussion has occurred only recently if at all.

Another problem confronting Orthodoxy—as it did other immigrant groups—was pluralism itself. How does *the* Orthodox Church conduct itself when it is in the midst of so many other churches, sects, and denominations? Does it hold itself aloof? Does it seek to make converts? Does it withdraw or condemn or ignore or cooperate? The ecumenical movement—that is, the movement toward greater cooperation and possible union of the separate churches—has intensified this question. Can Orthodoxy—after centuries of separate existence—reopen lines of communication and communion? A partial answer to that question was given in December, 1965, when Pope Paul VI of Rome and Patriarch Athenagoras I of Constantinople simultaneously lifted the excommunications that had been pronounced against each others' churches *nine centuries* earlier.

On Sunday, January 19, 1969, Archbishop Iakovos, the American head of the Greek Orthodox Church, preached in the Roman Catholic St. Patrick's Cathedral, New York City. This was an unprecedented event in America. Being without precedent, it provoked reaction and comment. Two excerpts are presented below, the first from Archbishop Iakovos' sermon on that occasion, the second a reaction from the prime archbishop, or Metropolitan Philaret of the Russian Orthodox Church Outside of Russia.

As you read about the issue of ecumenism[18] within Eastern Orthodoxy, consider the following questions and be prepared to discuss them:

1. Why would the question of relations with other churches be a "new " problem to most Orthodox immigrants?
2. What is the central theme of Archbishop Iakovos' message? To whom is he addressing this message? Why?
3. What is the basic argument of Metropolitan Philaret? Why does he oppose cooperation among different churches (i.e., ecumenism)? What role does "canon law" play? (You may want to consult an encyclopedia on the meaning of canon law.)
4. Do you feel that Iakovos anticipated the criticism of Philaret? If so, how?
5. Could one say that Philaret and Rabbi Schechter share concerns? Why or why not?

---

18 *Ecumenism*—the ecumenical movement; that is, the search for greater cooperation and possible union among the several churches and denominations of Christianity.

Archbishop Iakovos, head of the Greek Archdiocese of North and South America offered the benediction at the inaugural ceremony for President Lyndon B. Johnson in 1965.

6. How is the "dialogue" of Iakovos and Philaret illustrative of the problems facing other American churches? Can you give any examples?

Sermon by Archbishop Iakovos[19]

In the name of the Father and of the Son and of the Holy Spirit we are gathered here today, Christians of all persuasions, with one hope and prayer . . . This ecumenical observance, which has filled St. Patrick's . . . , has its real justification in our common wish to re-discover one another and to re-define our relationship with . . . God . . .

Oratorical definitions of Church Unity, accompanied by poetic, dramatic and romantic exhortation, will do nothing to further our desired goal of unity as long as the adherent to the faith does not commit himself to it. There is one clear definition which does justice to Church Unity. It is attributed to St. Epiphanius of Cyprus, and it goes as follows: "Though the Church be scattered all over the earth to

19 Taken from *The Greek Orthodox Observer* XXXV, February, 1969, pp. 6-7. Published by Greek Orthodox Archdiocese of North and South America.

the farthermost parts, she keeps the glad tidings diligently as though dwelling in one house. Thus the Churches throughout the world do not believe in anything different, nor are they teaching anything different . . . but in every place the gospel of salvation shines forth by its own self as the God created sun illuminates the whole world, yet being one himself."

I know of no better definition of Church Unity. But what this definition requires makes our task more difficult. Yet we all know from our Lord that "if we abide in Him and His words abide in us, we may ask whatever we will, and it shall be done for us" (John 15:7). If unity were an easy task, Christ would never have prayed for it, nor would have the Apostles and the Holy Fathers of the Church have so painfully concerned themselves with it. If we are sincere in our pursuit of unity, then we must clarify and define for our own benefit the true and full meaning of the specific mission that we as Christians have been assigned to fulfill. . . .

I am afraid that while we talk of Christian Unity, we add another inch to the walls of partition for the simple reason that we do not like even for the sake of Christ to reexamine our own confessional traditions and disciplines.

Who are those who impede and arrest the progress of Christian Unity? Those who are prayerfully studying the issues involved, or those who unashamedly arm themselves with the rusty weapons of hatred, stored by the bigots in the centuries-old arsenals of fanatic extremism? Who are those who are betraying the cause of Christian Unity? Those who are laboring for a renewed, vigorous and visionary Church or those who would prefer a divided, disunited, weak, an ineffective church, incapable of fulfilling the gospel, or reconciling men with one another and with God? . . .

My beloved fellow-brethren in Christ and my friends: when our astronauts at the risk of their lives try to build bridges between our planet and the moon; when our political leaders make use of every avenue to secure peace and unity in the world; when our Church leaders in the East and in the West travel thousands of miles in order to shorten inward distances between us; the least we can do is to see and understand Church Unity as a Divine Call, as a sacred duty and as the fulfillment of the gospel itself, of which we must be the servants. For Christianity, both as a theology and as a disciplined way of life has one ultimate goal: to bring about the unity and lead us into the blessed state of brotherly love which would efface unhappiness and suffering and bigotry from the eyes as well as from the hearts of men.

Letter from Metropolitan Philaret[20]

The following is the text of an open Letter to His Eminence Archbishop Iakovos, Greek Archdiocese of North and South America, from His Eminence Metropolitan[21] Philaret, Russian Orthodox Church Outside of Russia.

Your Eminence:

Many practices of our Church are based on precedent, and indeed the higher position of him who sets the precedent, the more important it is. Therefore, the ways that Orthodox bishops act in their contacts with the representatives of heterodox[22] confessions or religions are of special meaning. In those cases in which they deviate from the order accepted over the centuries, they cannot leave us indifferent. Our silence might be construed as consent, bringing consequent confusion to our own flock as well as misunderstanding to the heterodox expecting our actions . . . An incorrect action made by one bishop may be taken for something permitted by the whole Church, and those who are "without" may form a misconception in regard to Orthodox doctrine.

For this reason, the latest actions of Your Eminence . . . have greatly perplexed not only us and our flock, but also many others. We have in mind your recent participation at St. Patrick's Cathedral in the "Week of Prayer for Christian Unity," and the "Ecumenical Doxology" in the Greek Cathedral of the Holy Trinity.

The very fact that these services were publicized by the press as novelties with no precedent is indicative of their being introduced into the life of the church as something extraordinary and not properly pertaining to her nature. Which canon, what tradition gave you the right to introduce such novelties?

Orthodoxy by its implicit nature is marked by its fidelity to the tradition and example of Holy Fathers. . . .

In this case Your Eminence not only violated an ancient tradition of the Orthodox Church founded on [certain] canons but also in your actions and statements, conforming to those of Patriarch Athenagoras, you have expressed a teaching foreign to the Fathers of the Church. Orthodox ecclesiology[23] has always been based on the understanding that there is only One Holy, Catholic and Apostolic Church, and that

---

20 Taken from *St. Nectarios Educational Series #21* (Seattle, WA, n.d.).

21 *Metropolitan*—as a title in Eastern Orthodoxy, a bishop ranking just below the level of patriarch.

22 *Heterodox*—literally, "other opinion"; distinct and apart from orthodox.

23 *Ecclesiology*—the study of the nature and function of the church.

schismatics, heretics, and persons of other religions are outside of Her. We, therefore, cannot accept the assertion of His Holiness Patriarch Athenagoras . . . that ". . . the Church which was established by Christ to be glorious, without spot or wrinkle (Eph. 5:27), perfect and holy, was altered." If our Church was *altered* and is not the same that was established by our Savior,—[then] the One Holy, Catholic, and Apostolic Church . . . exists no more and instead there are several Churches, none of which is fully true and holy.

How sad it is to read of such rejection of the teachings of our Fathers in a message of the Primate of the Church which was the Mother of our Church of Russia! *You are uniting with the heterodox not in truth but in indifference for it.*

We are not writing these lines in order to simply reproach or offend Your Eminence or His Holiness Patriarch Athenagoras, not in the least, especially as we have no reason for personal animosity toward you or His Holiness.

On the contrary, we see as the duty of brotherly love our indicating to you and the Patriarch of the perils of Ecumenism which you have chosen.

Oh! If you would hearken to the calls of the Holy Fathers of the Church who did not build on compromises but on the firm adherence to the traditions and every iota of the divine dogmas—instead of to the voices of interconfessional conferences and the press indifferent to religious truth. Their true love toward the heterodox consisted of their zeal to enlighten them with the light of truth and in caring for their genuine reunion with the Holy Church.

We are writing this in an open letter since your statements were made public, and so that other Bishops and the faithful might know that not all the Church agrees with Your pernicious ecumenical ventures. Let it be clear to everyone that your [worship] with the heterodox is a unique episode which may not serve as a precedent or an example for others, but which causes concern and resolute protest on the part of devoted members of the Church as an action which is clearly unorthodox and in violation of the Holy Canons.

I am, Your obedient servant,
METROPOLITAN PHILARET

Day of Orthodoxy, 1969

The Orient in America

In 1893, the World Parliament of Religions met in Chicago, making it possible for many Americans to hear firsthand accounts of other major world religions besides Judaism and Christianity. Representatives came from India, China, Japan, the Near East, and many other places to tell of their own religious heritage and practice. Three world religions in particular won attention then and have maintained a presence in America ever since: Hinduism, Buddhism, and Islam.

Hinduism is so closely identified with the history, literature, and culture of India that it is impossible to speak of one without the other. Its origin hidden in the ancient past, Hinduism has a richness of scripture and ceremony that is difficult to export beyond its native land. Yet, some aspects of Hinduism do flourish in the United States, often associated with a particular spiritual teacher, or guru, and sometimes with a communal and colorful life style, an example of which is the Krishna Consciousness movement. Young members of this movement appear in saffron-colored robes, with shaved heads and painted faces, often begging for contributions and chanting, "Hare Krishna! Hare Rama!" (This is sometimes called "the great mantra," invoking the names "of the Supreme Lord.") A form of Hindu meditation called Transcendental Meditation aroused wide interest among many Americans in the late 1960s and on into the 1970s.

More truly mobile than Hinduism and therefore more truly a world or missionary religion, Buddhism first traveled from its native India throughout southeast Asia, into China, Korea, and Japan. When Christian missionaries reached these countries in the nineteenth century, Buddhist leaders often adopted western missionary techniques, creating (for example) Young Men's and Young Women's Buddhist Associations in imitation of the YMCA and YWCA. In Hawaii, Japanese Buddhism, which was officially established there in 1894, has grown to have great influence, and on the mainland of America, Buddhism has

Zen Buddhists engage in meditation called zazen, *also called "wall sitting" or "wall gazing."*

Shown here is the Islam Center on Massachusetts Avenue in Washington, D.C.

experienced considerable growth in the twentieth century. Though divided into many different ethnic and sectarian or denominational groups, the Buddhists all met in 1987 in the first American Buddhist Congress ever called together. Among the many purposes of the Congress, it was hoped that a day would be set aside to commemorate the birth, death, or enlightenment of the religion's founder who lived some six centuries before Christ. Also in 1987, the U.S. Armed Forces Chaplains Board agreed that the time had come to have Buddhist as well as Jewish and Christian chaplains to serve the approximately 2500 Buddhists in military services.

The youngest of the three religions discussed here, Islam, is also a vigorously missionary or world religion. Just as events in Vietnam highlighted the presence of Buddhist monks there, so events in the Middle East (Lebanon, Iran, Iraq, Saudi Arabia, etc.) have highlighted the presence of Moslems (and their denominational differences) in that part of the world. Arising in Arabia in the seventh century, Islam found its leadership in the prophet Muhammed and its inspiration in the Koran. Spreading quite rapidly in the first century of its existence, Islam for a time seemed destined to conquer all of Europe. It did conquer most of north

Africa and much of the territory between Arabia and India. Islamic Centers and distinctive mosques can now be found in most large cities in the United States, a particularly beautiful example of the characteristic Islamic architecture being the mosque in Washington, D.C.

In America, the presence of these venerable and deeply rooted religious traditions was matched by the presence of many new and possibly short-lived religious alternatives. The phrase "the new religions" covered a wide assortment of phenomena: some essentially Western, some principally Eastern, some combining elements from both East and West, and still others drawing only from the powerful presence of a single personality. The effect of the whole, however, was to make pluralism far more visible than it had ever been before; also, this varied whole made many people anxious about the nation's cultural or moral or religious oneness. An old and familiar motto in American history is *E Pluribus Unum,* "out of the many, one." That motto had originally applied to the thirteen colonies, of course, out of which the United States emerged in the 1780s. In the 1980s, however, many persons wondered whether the diversity had been stretched too far for any oneness to be found. We shall return to this issue at the end of the unit.

Patterns of Pluralism

Sometimes in America the number of churches and synagogues, mosques and temples, seem so numerous as to go beyond our comprehension. Students and sometimes scholars, too, throw up their hands in confusion and dismay. Is it possible to say anything about religion in America, or are the groups too many to permit anything but a catalog that will guide the perplexed through a great wilderness?

With respect to Judaism and Christianity, some help is provided in Table II, which gathers the largest (and perhaps most familiar) groups into twelve families. These twelve would account for about 90 percent of the church membership in the United States, though of course the term *family* should not be interpreted as standing for actual institutional unity.

About two thirds of all Americans are church members and in an average week about four out of every ten Americans attend some form of religious worship. While 40 percent church attendance may not seem all that high, the figure is much lower in most of the nations of Europe. According to Gallup polls, attendance is highest in the Midwest and the

South, lowest in the West. It is also somewhat lower among young people than among those more than fifty years of age. Though attendance records vary from year to year, the figure of 40 percent has been surprisingly stable for the last two decades.

As you examine Table II, determine the following:

1. What percentage of the *national population* is Protestant, Catholic, Jewish, and Eastern Orthodox?
2. What percentage of total *church membership* do these groups comprise?
3. Compare this information with Table I on page 154.
   a. What does this tell about the success of nativism?
   b. What generalizations could you make about the growth of the various denominations? What might account for the great changes in proportional strength?

Problems of Pluralism

Pluralism has its benefits, as it brings excitement and colorful variety into American life. It also has its problems, as it creates tension and often controversy in fields such as education and in questions regarding the use of religious symbols in public places. Many of the controversies find their way ultimately to the U.S. Supreme Court, which tries to interpret the precise meaning or application of the portion of the First Amendment that states that "Congress shall make no law respecting the establishment of religion or abridging the free exercise thereof."

What does the First Amendment mean? What does it require? What does it forbid? What did the original authors of the Amendment intend it to mean? These and similar questions have become part of the daily diet of Americans in recent years as society wrestles with questions such as prayer in the public schools, federal aid to sectarian private schools, Christmas decorations on city property, Sunday laws or regulations, brainwashing charges against certain religious groups, and so on. Since Americans are themselves divided on many of these issues, it is not surprising that the Justices of the Supreme Court do not always agree with each other about the constitutionality of any particular practice.

It is interesting to note that the Supreme Court has not always been so busy with religious questions as it has in recent years. In fact, for the first century and a half of our nation's history, the number of religion

TABLE II
Major Denominational Families in America

	FAMILY	MEMBERSHIP, 1985	% OF NATIONAL POPULATION
1.	Roman Catholic	52,655,000	22.0%
2.	Baptist[a]	25,612,000	11.0%
3.	Methodist[b]	13,398,000	5.0%
4.	Lutheran[c]	7,868,000	3.0%
5.	Pentecostal[d]	7,163,000	3.0%
6.	Mormon[e]	4,052,000	1.7%
7.	Christian[f]	3,771,000	1.5%
8.	Jewish[g]	3,750,000	1.5%
9.	Presbyterian (U.S.A.)	3,048,000	1.2%
10.	Orthodox[h]	2,950,000	1.2%
11.	Episcopal	2,739,000	1.1%
12.	United Church[i]	1,684,000	0.6%

a) Includes Southern Baptist Convention, American Baptist Churches, National Baptist Convention, National Baptist Convention, Inc., and Baptist Bible Fellowship.

b) Includes United Methodist Church, Christian Methodist Episcopal, African Methodist Episcopal, and African Methodist Episcopal Zion.

c) Includes American Lutheran Church, Lutheran Church in America, and Lutheran Church–Missouri Synod.

d) Includes Assemblies of God, Church of God in Christ, Church of God (Anderson), Church of God (Cleveland), United Pentecostal Church, and Church of the Foursquare Gospel.

e) Includes Church of Jesus Christ of Latter-day Saints (Utah) and Reorganized Church of Jesus Christ of Latter-day Saints (Missouri).

f) Includes Disciples of Christ, Churches of Christ, and Christian Churches.

g) Includes Reform, Conservative, and Orthodox branches of Judaism (estimated).

h) Includes only Greek and Russian Orthodox.

i) Represents the 1957 union of the Congregational Christian churches with the Evangelical and Reformed Church.

cases reaching the highest court was quite small. And the issues, with one exception, were not bitterly controversial. The one exception concerned the Church of Jesus Christ of Latter-day Saints, whose members practiced polygamy in the nineteenth century. In 1879 and again in 1890, the Supreme Court ruled that polygamy would not be allowed in any territory under the jurisdiction of the United States (see study 9). In the 1940s, the Supreme Court heard many free exercise cases related to the several activities of the Jehovah's Witnesses (also see study 9). Since that time, the Supreme Court has heard case after case, not necessarily related to any single religious group but to a variety of practices in the several states. And with each decision, the defining and the refining of the First Amendment has been advanced. But also, with many of these decisions, the anxiety or even the anger of large portions of the public have been evident.

Education has proved to be an especially troublesome area, both with respect to what may be taught or done in the public school and with respect to what may be supported or paid for by taxes in the private schools. Can the public schools offer voluntary sectarian instruction on the school grounds? No, ruled the Supreme Court in 1948. Can the public schools assist in making voluntary sectarian instruction possible off the school grounds? Yes, ruled the Supreme Court in 1952. Are prayer and Bible reading as classroom acts of worship constitutional in the public schools? In 1962 and 1963, the Court ruled that such actions were not consistent with "the Establishment Clause" of the First Amendment. These decisions created such dissent that efforts have been made ever since to pass a school prayer amendment to the Constitution or to remove such matters from the Supreme Court's decision-making powers. Many people did not notice that the 1963 decision also said that the academic *study* of religion was entirely constitutional and proper.

The 1962 case from the State of New York, *Engel* v. *Vitale*, concerned an official prayer composed by the Regents of the State to be recited in each classroom each morning. A portion of the Supreme Court's majority decision in this case is given below. As you read the decision, keep in mind the following questions:

1. What is meant by "the Establishment Clause"? (Re-read the portion of the First Amendment quoted in the first paragraph of this section.)
2. Why, in the Court's opinion, did the framers of the Constitution adopt this Amendment? Were they against religion? Did they worry about too much governmental power?

We think that by using its public school system to encourage repetition of the Regents' prayer, the State of New York has adopted a practice wholly inconsistent with the Establishment Clause. . . .

By the time of the adoption of the Constitution, our history shows that there was a widespread awareness among many Americans of the dangers of a union of Church and State. These people knew, some of them from bitter personal experience, that one of the greatest dangers to the freedom of the individual to worship in his own way lay in the Government's placing its official stamp of approval upon one particular kind of prayer or one particular form of religious service. . . . The First Amendment was added to the Constitution to stand as a guarantee that neither the power nor the prestige of the Federal Government would be used to control, support, or influence the kinds of prayer the American people can say—that the people's religions must not be subjected to the pressures of government. . . .

[Our Founders] knew that the First Amendment, which tried to put an end to governmental control of religion and of prayer, was not written to destroy either. . . . It is neither sacrilegious nor anti-religious to say that each separate government in this country should stay out of the business of writing or sanctioning official prayers and leave that purely religious function to the people themselves and to those the people choose to look to for religious guidance.[24]

In the realm of the sectarian private schools, the questions were chiefly financial. Who could or should pay for teacher's salaries, for the construction of buildings, for the purchase of textbooks, for vocational testing, for materials? As you can see, these matters could become complicated and detailed. Only one case was heard early in this century; the Supreme Court decided unanimously that the purchase of textbooks for use in sectarian private schools of the State of Louisiana was constitutional. But after World War II many, many cases came to the attention of the Supreme Court, and the nine Justices often found themselves arguing with each other. In a famous 1947 case that concerned the use of public buses to transport children to sectarian private schools, the Court was divided almost evenly, with five Justices approving the practice and four opposing it. Trying to make their way through a maze of difficult cases, the Justices asked themselves three questions with respect to any law that might seem to violate the First Amendment. First, did the law in question have a purpose that was primarily secular rather than religious? Second, did the law in its effect neither advance nor injure religion? And third, did the

24 R.T. Miller and R.B. Flowers, *Toward Benevolent Neutrality: Church, State, and the Supreme Court,* rev. ed. (Waco, TX: Baylor University Press, 1987), pp. 397-400.

law avoid any extreme or excessive entanglement between Church and State? If all three questions could be answered yes, then the law was said to pass the test of constitutionality, but these questions were not always easy to answer with total clarity or with total agreement.

One avenue explored for giving greater public support to sectarian private schools was what has been called the voucher plan. Under this plan, parents might receive an annual subsidy that could be paid to any school (public or private) of their choice. Or an alternate plan was to allow parents a tax credit of a stated amount that would help offset the tuition charges of the private schools. In a case coming from Minnesota, the Supreme Court in 1983 decided in a five-to-four decision that it was constitutional to allow parents a tax credit on expenditures for "tuition, textbooks, and transportation." A portion of the majority opinion in this case (*Mueller* v. *Allen*) follows. As you read the Supreme Court decision, consider the following questions:

1. In your opinion, why might it be difficult to draw a line between what is "established" (that is, government supported) and what is not?
2. What do you understand by the "TVA yardstick" (Tennessee Valley Authority)? Is this analogy useful? Is it convincing?

Today's case is no exception to our oft-repeated statement that the Establishment Clause presents especially difficult questions of interpretation and application. It is easy enough to quote the few words comprising that clause—"Congress shall make no law respecting an establishment of religion." It is not at all easy, however, to apply this Court's various decisions construing the Clause to governmental programs of financial assistance to sectarian schools and the parents of children attending those schools. Indeed, in many of these decisions "we have expressly or implicitly acknowledged that 'we can only dimly perceive the lines of demarcation in this extraordinarily sensitive area of constitutional law.'"

A state's decision to defray the cost of educational expenses incurred by parents—regardless of the type of schools their children attend—evidences a purpose that is both secular and understandable. An educated populace is essential to the political and economic health of any community, and a state's efforts to assist parents in meeting the rising cost of educational expenses plainly serves this secular purpose of ensuring that the state's citizenry is well-educated. Similarly, Minnesota, like other states, could conclude that there is a strong public interest in assuring the continued financial health of private schools, both sectarian and non-sectarian. By educating a substantial number of students such schools relieve public schools of a correspondingly great burden—to the benefit of all taxpayers. In addition, private schools may serve as a benchmark for public schools, in a manner analogous to the "TVA yardstick" for private power companies. As *Justice POWELL* has remarked: "Parochial schools, quite apart from their sectarian purpose, have provided an educational alternative for millions of young Americans; they often afford wholesome competition with our public schools; and in some States they relieve substantially the tax burden incident to the operation of public schools. The State has, moreover, a legitimate interest in facilitating education of the highest quality for all children within its boundaries, whatever school their parents have chosen for them."[25]

From what you have read in this section, it is perhaps clear that while pluralism offers many possibilities, it also presents some problems. It should also be clear that many of these problems have not been permanently settled or solved to the satisfaction of all Americans. Thus, you as future voters or office holders or concerned citizens will have both the opportunity and the responsibility to assist the nation as it finds its way down the pathways to pluralism.

25 R.T. Miller and R.B. Flowers, *Toward Benevolent Neutrality: Church, State, and the Supreme Court,* rev. ed. (Waco, TX: Baylor University Press, 1987), p. 553.

Index

Abbott, Lyman, 120, 122-123
Abolitionists, 77-82
Adams, John, 23
African Methodist Episcopal Church, 75
Alaska, 51
Allen, Richard, 73-75
America, 38-40
American Lutheran Church, 43
American Protective Association, 157-158
Amos, prophet, 104-105
Anglican Church. *See* Church of
    England
Anti-Defamation League, 171-172
Anti-Semitism, 168-174
Appeal to the Coloured Citizens of the
    World, 73
Appeal to the Public, 24-26
Applied Christianity, 105-106
Athenagoras I, Patriarch, 180
Ave Maria, 42-43

Baptists
  on the frontier, 52
  membership, 189
  number of churches, 154
  and slavery, 78-79
Barton, Thomas, 17-20
Beecher, Lyman, 60-61
Bishop of Landaff, letter to, 26-28
Bishops, Anglican, 22n., 23-28
Black Muslims, 84-85
Black Americans
  challenge to churches, 82-87
  church membership, 82
  "Free Africans," 73
  involuntary immigration, 72-73
  protest against Christianity, 80-82
  role of the church among, 74-76
Booth, Catherine, 99

Booth, Evangeline, 98
Booth, William, 99
Born to Battle, 99-101
Bryan, William Jennings, 123-124,
    126-128
Buber, Martin, 102-104
Buddhism, 185-187
Burger, Warren, 46, 47
Business and industry, 104-111, 111-114

Cabot, John, 9
Cabot, Sebastian, 9
Campbell, Alexander, 57
Canon Law, 159-162
Capers, William, 78
Cartwright, Peter, 62-63
Catholic Young Men's National Union, 99
Catholic Youth Organization, 99
Catholicism. *See* Roman Catholicism;
    Eastern Orthodoxy
Central Conference of American Rabbis,
    112-113
Challenging Years, 107-108
Chandler, Thomas Bradbury, 24-26
Chesham, Sallie, 99-101
Christendom, 9n.
Church membership, 154-155
Church of the Brethren, 10n., 152
Church of England, 17n., 23-28, 154
    See also Episcopalians
Church of Jesus Christ of Latter-day
    Saints. *See* Mormons
Churches of Christ, 189
Civil War, 77-80
Colleges, founded by churches, 65-67
Colonization, motives of, 3-10
Conformity, 12-13

Congregationalists *(continued)*
  on the frontier, 53
  number of churches, 154
  See also United Church of Christ
Conscience, definitions of, 136-138
Conscientious objection, 151-152
Constantine, Emperor, 36
Constitution, U.S., 142-152, 188-193
Conversion, 91-97
Copernicus, Nicolaus, 128, 128n.
Creationism, 129-132

Darrow, Clarence, 123-125
Darwin, Charles, 120
Dayton, Tennessee, 123
DeSmet, Pierre Jean, S.J., 63-65
Disciples of Christ (Christian)
  on the frontier, 57
  membership, 189
Discourse on Western Planting, 7-10
Dismissed time, 131
Douglass, Frederick, 80-82
Drake, Sir Francis, 5, 9

Eastern Orthodoxy, 155, 177-184, 189
Edwards v. *Aguillard,* 130-132
Elizabeth I, Queen, 4, 7
Elizabethtown, New Jersey, 24
Eller, Enten, 154
Engel v. *Vitale,* 190-191
Episcopalians
  on the frontier, 53
  membership, 189
  number of churches, 154
Establishment, religious, 18n., 24-35
Evangelism, 93n.

Far East religions, 185-187
Federal Council of Churches (National
    Council of Churches), 111-112
Finney, Charles G., 91-93
First Amendment, 35, 46-48, 139-152
Flag, saluting of, 142-150
Fosdick, Harry Emerson, 126, 128-129
Frankfurter, Felix, 143-145, 148-150
Frazier, E. Franklin, 76
Friar, 8n.
Friends, Society of. *See* Quakers
Frontier, U.S., 50-68
Furman, Richard, 78-79
Future of an American Jew, The, 171-174

Garnet, Henry Highland, 80
General Assembly of Virginia, 31-35

Gentile, 8n.
Gibbons, James Cardinal, 156, 160-162
Gilbert, Arthur, 169, 171-174
Gilbert, Sir Humphrey, 4-6
Gillette v. *United States,* 151-152
Gladden, Washington, 105-106
Gobitis, William and Lillian, 142
Gospel, 7n., 92n.
Graham, William F. (Billy), 94-97
Great Case of Liberty of Conscience, 14-16
Greek Orthodox, 178-184, 189
  See also Eastern Orthodoxy

Hakluyt, Richard, 7-10
Harris, Barbara, 86
Hasidism, 102-104
Hasidism and Modern Man, 102-104
Hebrew Union College, 58, 167
Henry, Patrick, 31-34
Hicks, Edward, 13
Hinduism, 185-187
Hispanic Catholics, 163-165
Hodge, Charles, 120-121

Iakovos, Archbishop, 180-182
Idolatry, 7-10
India, 185-187
Indians
  on the frontier, 63-65
  in the New World, 7-10
Individual, religion and, 90-103
Infidel, 8n.
Isaac, Jules, 170-171
Islam, 186-187

Jackson, Robert, 146-148
Jamestown, 7
Jefferson, Thomas, 36
Jehovah's Witnesses, 142-150
Jew in Christian America, A, 171-174
Jewish Theological Seminary, 168
Jews
  Americanization of, 167-168
  in the nation, 154
  increase of, 165-166
  on the frontier, 58-60
  prejudice against, 168-174
  population, 154-155, 189
  See also Judaism
Judaism
  Anti-Defamation League, 171
  Conservative, 166-167, 168
  on the frontier, 58-60
  Hasidic, 102-104

Orthodox, 166
Reconstructionism, 174-176
Reform, 58, 166-168
and social justice, 106-108, 112-113

Kaplan, Mordecai, 174-176
Kennedy, John F., 161
King, Martin Luther, Jr., 85-87
Knights of Columbus, 99
Ku Klux Klan, 84

Labor and industry, 106-114
Lancaster County (Pennsylvania), 17-18
Leo XIII, Pope, 113
Leprosaria, 100n.
Liberty Bell, 33
Liberty, religious, 14-20, 26-28, 31-35,
    138-150, 188-193
Livingston, William, 26-28
Louisiana Purchase, 50
Lutherans
    on the frontier, 54
    membership, 189
    number of churches, 154
    and tax policy, 43-44

Madison, James, 34-35
Malcolm X, 84-85
Marshall, Thurgood, 151-152
Masvidal, E.B., 164-165
Mather, Cotton, 22
Mayhew, Jonathan, 22
Memorial and Remonstrance, 34-35
Mennonites, 18
Methodists
    in colonial Pennsylvania, 18
    on the frontier, 54
    membership, 189
    number of churches, 154
    and slavery, 78
Mexican-Americans, 163-165
Middle East, 186-187
Minersville School District v. Gobitis (1940),
    143, 144-146
Moody, Dwight L., 93-94
Moravians, 18
Mormons (Church of Jesus Christ of
    Latter-day Saints)
    on the frontier, 57-58
    membership, 189
    migrations of, 139
    and the U.S. Supreme Court, 139-142
Moslems, 186-187
Moss, Joan, 101-102

Motivation, analysis of, 2-3
Mueller v. Allen, 192-193

National Association for the
    Advancement of Colored People,
    106
National Catholic Welfare Conference
    (United States Catholic Conference),
    113n.
National Conference of Christians and
    Jews, 44-45
National Hispanic Pastoral Encuentro,
    164-165
Nativism, 155-162
Nature, approaches to, 118-119
Newfoundland, map of, 5
Nixon, Richard, 95

O'Connor, Sandra Day, 131
Oriental influences, 185-187
Our Country, 159-160
Overstreet, H.A., 169, 174

Paraguay, 101-102
Pastoral Letter (1833), 157
Paul VI, Pope, 180
Peck, John Mason, 61, 78-79
Penn, William, 14-16
Pennsylvania, 14
Pentecostal, 189
Persecution, religious, 14-16, 138-142
Philaret, Metropolitan, 183-184
Plea for the West, A, 60-61
Pluralism, 187-193
Polish Catholics, 163
Politics, religion and, 107-108
Polygamy, 138-142
Presbyterians
    in colonial Pennsylvania, 18
    on the frontier, 55
    membership, 189
    number of churches, 154
    and slavery, 79
    and tax policy, 40-42
Protestantism
    in colonial America, 24-28
    growth of, 154
    and infallibility, 16
    and social gospel, 105-106, 111-112
    "true and sincere religion," (Hakluyt), 8
    versus Roman Catholicism, 155-162
    See also individual denominations
Psalms, Book of, 118

Quakers (Society of Friends)
  in colonial Pennsylvania, 18
  in England, 14
  on the frontier, 55
  and slavery, 76

Raleigh, Sir Walter, 3-4
Randolph, A. Phillip, 83
Reconstructionism, 174-176
Reformed Churches, Dutch and
  German, 154
Rehnquist, William, 131
Revivalism
  on the frontier, 62-63
  and the individual, 90
  See also individual revivalists
Revolutionary War, 23, 26
Reynolds v. *United States* (1879), 140-142
Roman Catholicism
  conversion of the Indians, 7-8
  on the frontier, 56, 57
  Hispanic, 163-165
  membership, 189
  and nativism, 158-162
  number of churches, 154
  and social action, 108-111, 113-114
  and tax policy, 38-40, 42-43
Russell, Charles Taze, 142
Russian Orthodox, 178-180
  See also Eastern Orthodoxy
Ryan, John A., 108-111

Sabbath, 91n.
Salt Lake City, 58
Salvation, 91n.
Salvation Army, the, 97, 102
San Xavier del Bac Mission, 56
Scalia, Antonin, 131
Schechter, Solomon, 166, 168
Science, religion and
  in evolution controversy, 120-132
  at war, 119
Scopes, John T., 123, 124, 126
Sects, 18n.
Slave trade, 76-77
Slavery
  division of the denominations, 78-80
  a reproach to Christianity, 80-82
Smith, Joseph, 57-58
Social Reconstruction, 109-111

Society, religion and, 104-115
Society for the Propagation of the
  Gospel, 17-20
Society of St. Vincent de Paul, 99
Spirituals (Negro), 70-72
Stanley, David S., 63-65
Stone, Barton, 57
Stone, Harlan, 145-146
Strong, Josiah, 156, 158-160
Supreme Court, U.S.
  evolution and the churches, 129-132
  and the Jehovah's Witnesses, 142-150
  and the Mormons, 138-142
  taxing the churches, 46-48
Synagogues
  in colonial America, 154
  in 1850, 59

Taxation and the churches, 36-48
Teaching of Contempt, The, 170-171
Totem pole, 51

United Church of Christ, 189

Vatican Council II, 169
Voucher Plan, 192-193

Waite, Morrison R., 140-142
Walker, David, 73
Walz, Frederick, 46
Walz v. *Tax Commission*, 46-48
War Cry, 101-102
West, Benjamin, 14
West Virginia State Board of Education v.
  Barnette (1943), 143, 146-150
What is Darwinism?, 120-121
White, Andrew D., 119
White, Byron, 131
Wise, Isaac Mayer, 58, 166-168
Wise, Stephen S., 106-108
Women's suffrage, 150

Young, Brigham, 58
Young Men's Christian Association,
  98-99
Young Women's Christian Association,
  98-99
Young Men's Hebrew Association, 99
Young Women's Hebrew Association, 99